EastEnders

Annual 2009

Tim Randall

BBC
BOOKS

Published in 2008 by BBC Books,
an imprint of Ebury Publishing.
A Random House Group Company.

10 9 8 7 6 5 4 3 2 1

Main text by Tim Randall
Copyright © Woodlands Books Limitied 2008

BBC Books would like to thank Diederick Santer, Carolyn
Weinstein, Samantha Denton, Rebecca Wojciechowski and
the Eastenders production team for all their help in compiling
this book.

The Random House Group Limited Reg. No. 954009

Address for companies within the Random House Group can be
found at www.randomhouse.co.uk

A CIP catalogue record for this book is available from the British
Library.

ISBN 978 1 846 07555 1

The Random House Group Limited supports The Forest
Stewardship Council (FSC), the leading international forest
certification organisation. All our titles that are printed on
Greenpeace approved FSC certified paper carry the FSC logo.
Our paper procurement policy can be found at
www.rbooks.co.uk/environment.

Commissioning Editor: Lorna Russell
Project Editor: Eleanor Maxfield
Art Direction & Design: Lockwood & Son
Picture Researcher: Esther Barry

Colour reproduction by Altaimage
Printed and bound in Italy by Graphicom Srl.

To buy books from your favourite authors and register for offers,
visit www.rbooks.co.uk

EastEnders

Annual 2009

Tim Randall

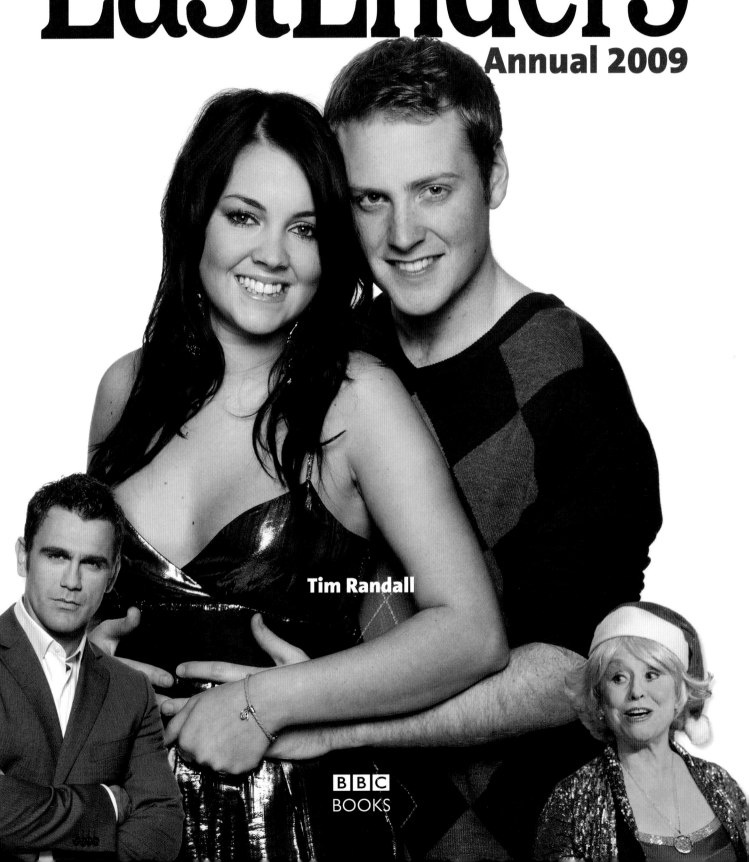

BBC
BOOKS

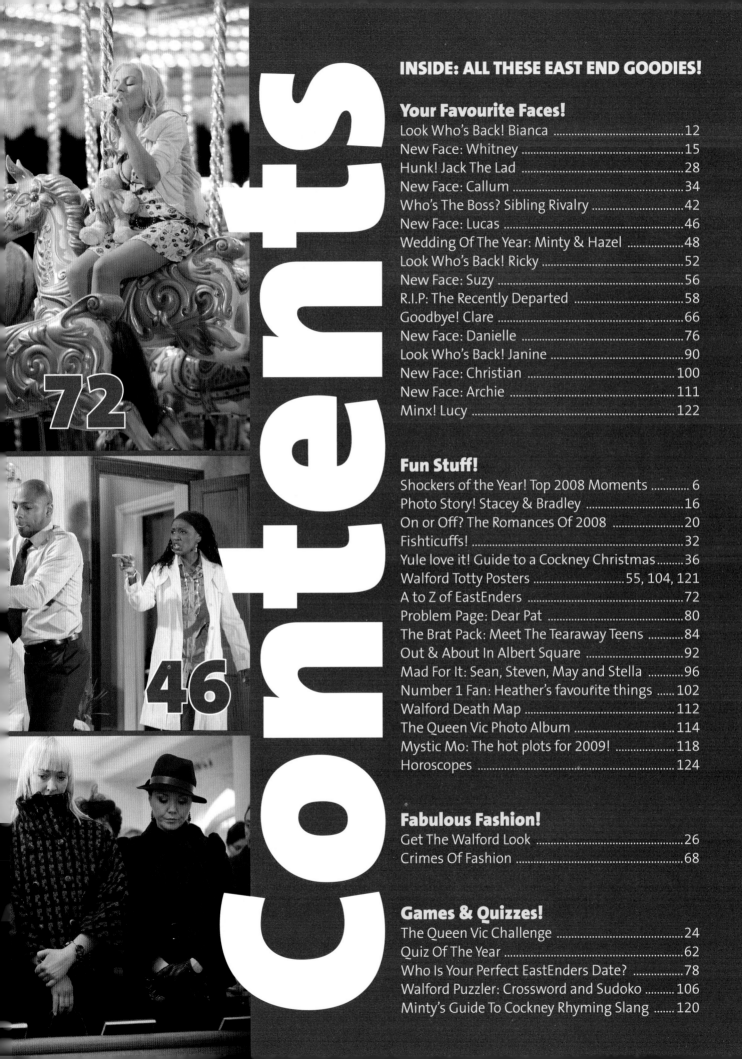

Contents

72

46

INSIDE: ALL THESE EAST END GOODIES!

Your Favourite Faces!
Look Who's Back! Bianca 12
New Face: Whitney 15
Hunk! Jack The Lad 28
New Face: Callum 34
Who's The Boss? Sibling Rivalry 42
New Face: Lucas 46
Wedding Of The Year: Minty & Hazel 48
Look Who's Back! Ricky 52
New Face: Suzy 56
R.I.P: The Recently Departed 58
Goodbye! Clare 66
New Face: Danielle 76
Look Who's Back! Janine 90
New Face: Christian 100
New Face: Archie 111
Minx! Lucy 122

Fun Stuff!
Shockers of the Year! Top 2008 Moments 6
Photo Story! Stacey & Bradley 16
On or Off? The Romances Of 2008 20
Fishticuffs! 32
Yule love it! Guide to a Cockney Christmas 36
Walford Totty Posters 55, 104, 121
A to Z of EastEnders 72
Problem Page: Dear Pat 80
The Brat Pack: Meet The Tearaway Teens 84
Out & About In Albert Square 92
Mad For It: Sean, Steven, May and Stella 96
Number 1 Fan: Heather's favourite things 102
Walford Death Map 112
The Queen Vic Photo Album 114
Mystic Mo: The hot plots for 2009! 118
Horoscopes 124

Fabulous Fashion!
Get The Walford Look 26
Crimes Of Fashion 68

Games & Quizzes!
The Queen Vic Challenge 24
Quiz Of The Year 62
Who Is Your Perfect EastEnders Date? 78
Walford Puzzler: Crossword and Sudoko 106
Minty's Guide To Cockney Rhyming Slang 120

SHOCKERS
OF THE YEAR

EXPLOSION!
JASE & MICKEY
RESCUE BABY
SUMMER

18 JUNE 2008

E20's deranged Dr May made her second attempt to steal baby Summer from Dawn this year – but only succeeded in blowing up the Millers' house and topping herself in the process. However, before the disgraced doctor was carried out in a body-bag, she found time to crack Mickey's skull with a conveniently placed crowbar. Luckily, Mickey regained consciousness and managed to lock himself, Dawn and Summer in a bedroom before fainting again. Meanwhile, May popped into the kitchen for a much-needed cigarette beside an open gas oven. In the Square, the gathered throng watched on as smoke billowed out of the burning terrace with Dawn trapped inside and Mickey hanging lifelessly from an upstairs window. It was up to unlikely hero Keith to save the day...

TANYA FIGHTS BACK!

TANYA'S REVENGE! MAX IS DRUGGED AND BURIED ALIVE

FANCY A TRIP TO THE WOODS?

21 MARCH 2008

After being pushed over the edge by a combination of Max's affair with droopy-drawers Stacey and his dirty tricks campaign during their divorce proceedings, Tanya decided to take drastic measures to get Max out of her life for good – by burying him alive in the Walford woods.

Having drugged him and dumped him in a freshly dug grave, her ever-helpful accomplice Sean Slater was just about to finish Max off with a shovel when Tanya stopped him, explaining she wanted Max to be buried alive as he'd once confided that his worst childhood memory was of being locked overnight in a coffin by drunk dad Jim.

When Max came round enough to beg Tanya to stop, she slid the lid on the coffin and covered it with earth, leaving a terrified Max to his worst nightmare. But, luckily for him, back home Tanya became frantic with guilt, drove back to the woods and dragged her spluttering husband out of the ground. On the downside, she then had to fight him off as he tried to strangle her...

WHO MADE PAT ANGRY?

9

CLEAN OR DIRTY!?

A LOAD OF PANTS — HOPALONG PAT ATTACKS SHIRLEY!

13 MAY 2008

When Heather arrived back from honeymoon, Shirley was determined to find out whether her best mate and hubby Minty had actually 'done the deed' – so she turned up at the launderette with a bottle of vodka to loosen Heather's tongue. As the booze kicked in, the bladdered twosome began rummaging through the service-wash laundry and came across some very saucy lingerie indeed. They cracked up when it turned out they were fingering Pat Evans' lacy smalls – which were actually anything but small – until an unamused Pat popped in, realised it was her underwear on display and swiftly whacked Shirley to the floor with one of her crutches!

GOT A PROBLEM? PAT DISHES OUT HER ADVICE ON PAGE 80

'Do you think
one long
I left

PAT'S QUIET LIFE ON THE SQUARE WAS RUDELY INTERRUPTED THIS YEAR BY THE RETURN OF A CERTAIN FOG-HORN-VOICED RELATIVE…

One sixth of the Jackson family, who arrived on Albert Square in 1993, red-haired and fiery tempered Bianca cemented E20's fate as the noisiest postcode in the UK. After six years of screaming, screeching and wailing her way from one disaster to another, Bianca left her London home in disgrace – having cheated on husband Ricky with her mum's new fella, Dan Sullivan.

Away from Walford she managed to create an army of kids and a stepchild from various boyfriends over the years. Faced with having them taken away from her and put into care, she sought refuge with her nana Pat and ex-husband Ricky and swiftly bundled her belongings into plastic bags, heading back to the place she once called home, which was now awash with Branning family members.

Time hadn't mellowed Bianca though. Every bit as argumentative as she was in her teens, she soon made fresh enemies with those who'd strayed onto her former patch. Grant and Natalie might be long gone, but she found new adversaries in the form of Stacey Slater, Zainab Masood and Jane Beale – the latter of whom got a faceful of breaded haddock when she dared to disrespect Bianca during the Walford Fishmonger's annual bash.

This time around, Bianca has new priorities though: her kids. Liam, Tiff, Morgan, and stepdaughter Whitney, are her number one priority and after her partner Tony ended up in prison for GBH, she was holding the rabble together single-handedly. Taking inspiration from mum Carol, Bianca's

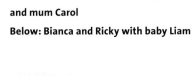

Above: Three's a crowd – Bianca, Dan and mum Carol

Below: Bianca and Ricky with baby Liam

'The word rude was invented for that woman!'

Zainab Masood

life's just been laugh since Walford?'

Hello daddy! Bianca and David in 1994

Shoplifting and vandalism aside, for most of the time they fall into line and always have food on their plates – so long as the Minute Mart doesn't run out of chicken nuggets.

mothering methods fall under the belief that the louder you scream, the harder it is for your kids to ignore you.

Bianca was counting down the days until Tony got released from the big house – but just how close is Tony's bond to Whitney and what secrets will Bianca uncover now he's back? And if they get uncovered, will her life be left in the traditional shambolic mess? Whatever the outcome, her future on the Square is bound to involve more screaming.

Below: The Jacksons party at Dot's

SEE BIANCA AND JANE'S FISH FIGHT **ON PAGE 32!**

TOP 5 WALFORD GINGERS

1. BIANCA Her barnet's tangeriney but Bianca's anything but sweet!

2. BRADLEY All the ladies want a feel of Bradley's carrot top

3. TIFFANY Like fellow redhead Anne Robinson there's a dark side to little Tiffany...

4. MAX Unlike a Duracell battery, copper-topped Max's pulling power is running out

5. SEAN Basil Brush and Mad Sean Slater. Separated at birth?

THE BRANNING FAMILY TREE

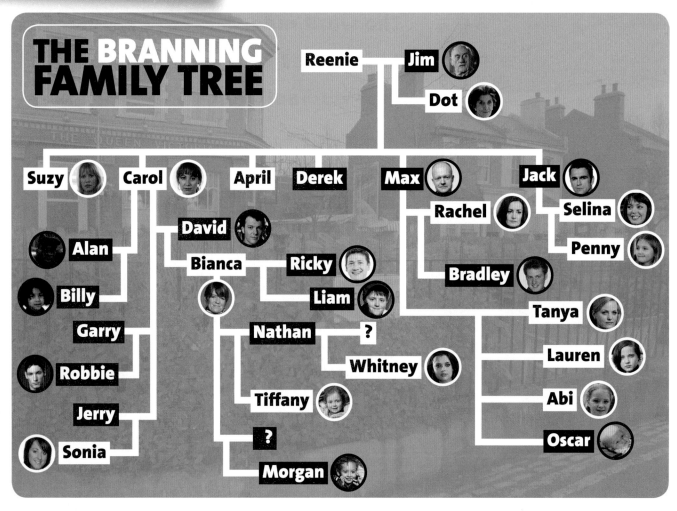

Reenie — Jim — Dot

Suzy — Carol — April — Derek — Max — Jack

Alan
Billy
Garry
Robbie
Jerry
Sonia

David
Bianca

Ricky
Liam

Nathan — ?
Whitney
Tiffany
?
Morgan

Rachel
Selina
Penny
Bradley
Tanya
Lauren
Abi
Oscar

WHITNEY DEAN:
Teen Queen

If ever there was someone who could tell Bianca to shut it without getting a mouthful or a smack round the chops – it's Whitney Dean. There seems to be a mutual respect between the savvy teenager and her feisty stepmum, which perhaps isn't that surprising when you look at what they've been through together.

Her dad Nathan was tragically killed in a road accident when she was only ten years old and at the same time Bianca was pregnant with their cheeky-faced offspring Tiffany. It seems the pair's shared grief bonded them for ever and Bianca took Whitney in, not only thinking of her as one of her own, but also as a mate and confidante.

Like most Walford teens, Whitney hasn't been averse to a spot of shoplifting or sulky gobbiness, but her heart is in the right place as she demonstrated when she begged Vinnie for ownership of Wellard to cheer up little Tiff. So when Whitney became withdrawn and distant soon after Tony was released from jail, Bianca and Pat began to worry about what was getting her down. But their fears over what could be wrong are nowhere near as shocking as the truth...

Who are you calling a Chav?
Whitney Dean arrives
in Walford

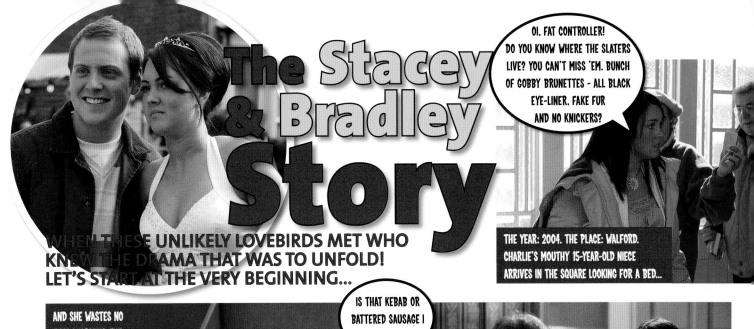

The Stacey & Bradley Story

WHEN THESE UNLIKELY LOVEBIRDS MET WHO KNEW THE DRAMA THAT WAS TO UNFOLD! LET'S START AT THE VERY BEGINNING...

THE YEAR: 2004. THE PLACE: WALFORD. CHARLIE'S MOUTHY 15-YEAR-OLD NIECE ARRIVES IN THE SQUARE LOOKING FOR A BED...

SHE'S A RIGHT LITTLE TROUBLEMAKER THIS ONE

THEY SEEM REALLY PLEASED TO SEE ME - I THINK I'M GONNA LIKE IT HERE!

MO AND CHARLIE AREN'T EXACTLY CHUFFED TO SEE HER BUT STACEY SOON MAKES HERSELF AT HOME...

YOU CAN JUST STAY FOR TONIGHT, STACEY. I MEAN IT. ONE NIGHT ONLY...

THIS IS BETTER THAN PRACTISING ON MY ARM

AT LAST - A WALFORD BLOKE WHO BRUSHES HIS TEETH

SLURP! SLURP! MMMM!

SLURP! SLURP! AAAAAH!

DESPITE SEVERAL DATING MISHAPS THE PAIR FALL IN LOVE - ALTHOUGH THEIR ATTEMPTS TO SLEEP TOGETHER ARE DISASTROUS...

GET A FEW PINTS OF SNAKEBITE DOWN YER NECK FIRST, SON. THAT ALWAYS WORKS FOR ME AND DOROTHY

LUCKILY WISE OLD JIM IS ON HAND TO OFFER SOME GRANDFATHERLY ADVICE...

I AINT DOIN' PHIL MITCHELL

BRADLEY'S NOT RIGHT FOR YOU. YOU NEED SOMEONE OLDER WITH MORE CASH. AND POSSIBLY BALD...

BUT MOTHERHOOD ISN'T TO BE FOR STACEY AFTER EVIL MAX'S INTERFERENCE...

YOU FINK YOU'RE BETTER THAN ME? BOVVERED! I GOT FARTS MORE INTERESTING THAN YOU LOT

A DRUNK STACEY EMBARRASSES BRADLEY WHEN SHE TURNS UP UNINVITED AT HIS WORK DO - SO HE DUMPS HER...

LOOK WHAT MAX GAVE ME FOR CHRISTMAS...

THAT'S NOTHING COMPARED TO WHAT HE GAVE ME EARLIER

STACE, YOUR EFFERVESCENT PERSONALITY AND SUNNY SMILE LIGHT UP MY LIFE. WILL YOU MARRY ME?

WHATEVER...

AS THEIR AFFAIR CONTINUES A STROPPY STACEY PUTS PRESSURE ON MAX TO LEAVE WIFE TANYA...

IN JULY UNAWARE SHE'S ALSO COPPING OFF WITH HIS DAD BRADLEY PROPOSES TO STACEY - SHE ACCEPTS...

BRIDE-TO-BE STACEY TRIES ON MO'S KNOCKOFF WEDDING DRESSES...

AND SHE GIVES MUM JEAN THE SHOCK OF HER LIFE...

UNDETERRED EVIL MAX DECLARES HIS LOVE FOR STACEY AT THE WEDDING REHEARSAL...

BUT AS THE JOYFUL CELEBRATIONS GET UNDERWAY...

...EVIL MAX AND STACEY CAN'T KEEP THEIR HANDS OFF EACH OTHER

AND NEITHER DOES A DEVASTATED BRADLEY WHO BATTERS SANTA/MAX....

IT FINALLY DAWNS ON EVIL MAX THE DESTRUCTION HE HAS CAUSED...

IN FEBRUARY STACEY BEGS BRADLEY FOR ANOTHER CHANCE AT A DR WHO CONVENTION - BUT HE TELLS HER IT IS OVER...

A BROKEN-HEARTED STACEY DECIDES TO MOVE ON AND DATE SOMEONE WITHOUT ANY BAGGAGE - ERM, STEVEN BEALE...

19

♥N OR ♥FF?

WHO HAD THE HOTS FOR EACH OTHER AND WHOSE RELATIONSHIPS BLEW COLD THIS YEAR? HERE WE GIVE YOU THE LURVE LOWDOWN...

♥ON!

PEGGY & ARCHIE MITCHELL

At last – Peggy has finally bagged herself a new fella and when they get married she won't even have to change her name. A handsome pair of veteran lovebirds they make too. But on the downside, we wouldn't trust manipulative Archie as far as we could throw him and he's lovin' being head of the Mitchell clan a little too much for our liking. When it comes to mind games, that man could outfox Derren Brown!

♥OFF!

BIANCA JACKSON & RICKY BUTCHER

Much as Ricky would like to take Bianca up the aisle yet again, she's been waiting for Tony to get out of prison and it's been the last thing on her mind to rekindle relations with her dopey ex-husband. But surely it's only a matter of time before one of Walford's greatest double acts are reunited...

♥ON!

JANE & IAN BEALE

They've had more ups and downs than the London Eye but even the devious mind of Clare Bates couldn't split up the Beales this year. Clare led Ian on by flirting and licking her lips a lot while wearing her trademark minimal clothing around him. But it was all just a game to her and she had no intention of taking things further. She then blackmailed Ian, threatening to inform Jane of his dishonourable intentions unless he gave her money. In the end, a panicked Ian came clean to a furious Jane, who then 'accidentally' spilled her drink all over the blackmailing bint.

OFF!

LUCY BEALE & OLLY GREENWOOD

Runaway Lucy met crusty hippy Olly when she was homeless and swiftly moved him in Chez Beale in order to wind up dad Ian. But *Teletubbies* fan Olly was soon thrown out and Christian's flat became their very own private love nest. However, Lucy's dreams of rebelling with a 'bit of rough' stoner boyfriend were shattered in August when she met Olly's mum and it turned out he was actually quite posh – so she dumped him.

OFF!

HEATHER TROTT & MINTY PETERSON

From what started as a bonkers scam to win the wedding competition, Heather fell in love with Minty. But after Hazel Hobbs' unexpected return, the cheese-loving optimist admitted defeat and tearfully got on a bus to leave Walford for good. But Minty rushed to stop her, proclaiming: 'I just want someone I can sit on the sofa with and watch *The Goonies* on a Sunday afternoon. Will you marry me, Heather?' Put like that, how could she refuse? But after spending a honeymoon in separate beds and Minty snogging a blonde bimbo stewardess, Heather finally realised what she'd probably known all along: that Minty loved her as a mate but he didn't love her as a wife.

♥FF!
HONEY & BILLY MITCHELL

Their first wedding was postponed when Honey was admitted to hospital with food poisoning, they failed to tie the knot at their second attempt thanks to a stag-night prank and third time around Honey's waters broke – but this time it was after she had said 'I do'. The couple's split was equally dramatic – after learning that Billy had taken blood money from Jase's death, a shocked Honey couldn't trust him anymore and left Walford, taking their children with her.

♥N!
LIBBY FOX & DARREN MILLER

This pair of level-headed teens celebrated their first year together in May, but ended up rowing when Jay revealed Darren's secret stash of specialist 'adult' mags. Libby was furious and ended up confiding in Tamwar Masood, with whom she'd just set up a home tutoring business, which made Darren very jealous. After finding suspect messages on Libby's phone he convinced himself the fellow swots were having an affair and soon it all seemed to be turning into an episode of *Gossip Girl* – only less glamourous. Eventually the pair realised they'd overreacted and began thinking about taking their relationship to the next level. This plan was again thwarted by eavesdropping prankster Jay Brown and resulted in Libby getting sozzled – with Chelsea's help – and promptly throwing up outside *R&R*. Thankfully, despite all of this, our favourite Walford teens are still very much an item!

♥FF!
SHIRLEY CARTER & VINNIE MONKS

Romance blossomed for this mismatched twosome when newcomer Vinnie's car knocked Shirley over while she was on her way to court for Deano's trial. A difficult nut to crack, nice-guy Vinnie didn't give up on Shirl despite the fact she was more interested in making an insurance claim against him than making out. But eventually the hard-faced barmaid did succumb to Vinnie's cheeky-chappie charms, they moved into a flat together and love seemed to be in the air. However, it wasn't long before the cab-driver realised it was Phil that Shirley was always going to be more interested in and sick of feeling like second best to Mr Potato Head – he finished it and the couple went their separate ways.

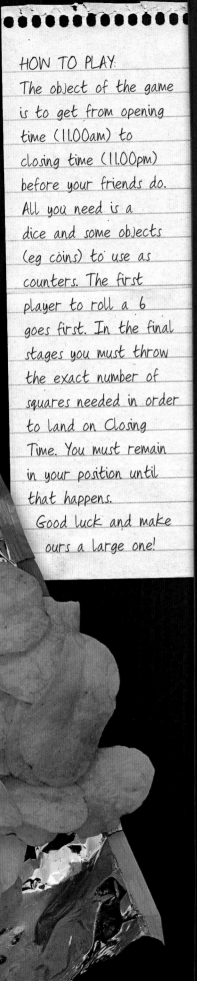

HOW TO PLAY:

The object of the game is to get from opening time (11.00am) to closing time (11.00pm) before your friends do. All you need is a dice and some objects (eg coins) to use as counters. The first player to roll a 6 goes first. In the final stages you must throw the exact number of squares needed in order to land on Closing Time. You must remain in your position until that happens.

Good luck and make ours a large one!

24

TOILETS

I CAN'T DECIDE BETWEEN WHAM RAP AND YOUNG GUNS!

HEATHER WANTS YOUR HELP CHOOSING A FLOORFILLER. MEET HER AT THE JUKEBOX

YOU'VE PULLED! MOVE FORWARD TO 19.00

A FLIRTY CALLUM SAYS YOU'VE GOT BEAUTIFUL EYES AND BUYS YOU A BAG OF PORK SCRATCHINGS

THE Queen

STROPPY SHIRLEY STARTS HER SHIFT AND SHORT-CHANGES YOU. GO BACK TO 12.30

YOU GAVE ME A FIVER NOT A TENNER - NOW HOPPIT!

THE QUEEN VICTORIA

IT'S SO NICE TO HAVE SOMEONE TO CHAT TO!

YOU GET STUCK WITH CHARLIE WHO REGALES YOU WITH THE HISTORY OF LONDON CABBIES (1897 ONWARDS). MISS A GO!

THIS IS WALFORD NOT FLIPPIN BENIDORM!

DARTBOARD

IT'S LUNCHTIME BUT RONNIE REFUSES TO SERVE YOU WHEN YOU TRY TO PAY IN EUROS. GO BACK AND START AGAIN!

Roxy

You can take the girl out of Ibiza, but you can't take Ibiza out of a girl's wardrobe and this mish-mash of influences shows creativity if nothing else. There's a hint of Paris, a dash of Posh and a nod towards Kate Moss, which is very impressive when you consider the only place to shop is Bridge Street Market.

Wild West meets the East End. Perch a big hat on your head and no-one need notice you haven't brushed your hair for a week.

Brighten up any outfit with a large piece of fruit. Bananas are a no-no though.

Roxy may not be posh but these frills are very Victoria Beckham. Pity Sean's no David.

Get The Walford Look

EVER WONDERED HOW THE RESIDENTS OF E20 KEEP ONE STEP AHEAD IN THE FASHION STAKES? HERE'S OUR GUIDE TO DRESSING LIKE A TRUE EASTENDER...

The strappy Roman sandal look is big this year, and as Roxy demonstrates, it gives you the chance to show off your recent pedicure.

Bradley

Bradley's style is straight out of a catalogue. Unfortunately the catalogue is from 1986 but that's not to say he doesn't wear it with a certain panache. Best of all, it's easy to get the look (should you want to).

Stripes tend to make most people look wider than they are, but Bradley needs all the beefing up he can get. And the yellow clashes nicely with his hair...

Nothing says 'mild-mannered librarian' like brown cords but on the plus side they don't need ironing!

On anyone else, rainbow-coloured knitwear would be overkill, but on Heather a muff works a treat.

Heather

The launderette worker has clearly thrown out all her mirrors if she's leaving the house looking like this. Having said that, full marks for creating a unique and brave look. Heather, we salute you!

This furry pouch is cheaper than a pet but just as cuddly!

TO HAT OR NOT TO HAT

When it comes to effortlessly cool style, no-one does it quite like Patrick Trueman, who is famed for his 'trilby at a jaunty angle' signature look. Here we've made a few alternative headpiece suggestions for E20's Mr Smooth...

This woolly baby blue beanie is perfect for the Walford winter ski season...

Ooh la la! If Patrick pops across the channel to Paris, this beret could be tres a la mode.

He'll have no excuse for not getting his five portions of fruit a day in this head-turner!

Jack
THE LAD

Since arriving on Albert Square Jack Branning has sent Walford's hormone levels soaring. The square-jawed beef-cake has saved the area's ailing sex appeal, where previously the likes of Garry Hobbs and Minty Peterson were the closest thing to an eligible gentleman. Being an ex-copper didn't seem to put off the local talent, and quicker than you could say 'Sorry Mickey, I'm washing my hair,' the ladies were queuing round the block for a slice of Branning action.

It was ice queen Ronnie Mitchell who turned fitness fanatic Jack's head at first – and they started the year having enjoyed a seasonal snog.

But like any member of the Branning clan, Jack doesn't come without baggage. The arrival of Jack's former wife, Selina, broke up his burgeoning relationship with Ronnie when Jack enjoyed a secret night of passion with his ex for old times' sake. Only it wasn't quite as secret as Jack had hoped for when Roxy spilled the beans and promptly trashed the love rat's beloved soft furnishings as revenge for her sister.

While Ronnie ran hot and cold over her feelings, Jack got himself into further trouble when he grew confused as to which Mitchell he fancied (aka 'Sharon Watts syndrome') and slept with Roxy. Equally as blonde, but ≫→

Loverboy Jack with the many women in his life: Roxy, Ronnie and Tanya

without the class of her older sister, it's a night Jack is desperate to forget – not realising that her baby could be his (while he's a whiz at biology, maths isn't a strong subject for Jack, clearly).

Adding to Jack's reservations about Ronnie was her frosty relationship with his daughter Penny. Clearly dealing with maternity issues of her own, Ronnie didn't bond with wheelchair-bound Penny as Jack had hoped and it proved a stumbling block in their ever-difficult romance.

It's not just the female Mitchells

Jack wiith daughter Penny

that Jack's been toying with – his ongoing rivalry with Phil has been a constant headache for him. The ex-con and the ex-copper were probably never destined to be best buddies, and it's no surprise that Jack's investment in the R&R club rubbed Phil up the wrong way.

The former hard man of Albert Square may have met his match in Jack, who always seems to come

JACK'S REIGN OVER THE MAN-HUNGRY POPULATION OF E20 CEMENTS HIM AT THE THERE ARE SEVERAL OTHER PRETENDERS TO THE HEART-THROB THRONE, ALL WITH

Lotharios!

Max
He may not have the model looks of his brother, but that's never stopped sex-mad Max getting his wicked way with the local talent. Stealing his son Bradley's fiancée Stacey is his most shocking achievement to date.

Sean
Sean's red hot sex appeal means his conquests to date have included Ruby, Preeti, Carly, Chelsea, Tanya and Roxy. He might be as mad as a box of frogs, but he's certainly got a way with the ladies.

Christian
Barely a morning goes by in Walford without Christian rocking up to the café with last night's bleary-eyed arm candy by his side. Never one to indulge in anything further than a one-night stand, Christian even managed to attract loopy emo Steven Beale, but turned him down gracefully. Well, even Christian's got some standards.

Callum
The latest stud on the Square is the unlikely product of hapless Vinnie's loins. Like father, like son – as Vinnie homed in on ageing good-time girl Shirley, Callum's smitten with droopy-drawers herself, Stacey Slater. With Callum's looks we suspect she'll be the first of many.

out on top. Given the trauma of getting involved with the Mitchell clan, it's little wonder that Jack turned his attentions to a much simpler project – that of stealing his brother Max's family. While Max remained in exile following his minibreak in a coffin in Walford Woods, Jack moved in on Tanya and her cosy life with her three kids. Tanya, presumably thrilled to find a man who won't cheat on her with the

Is the pressure getting to Mr Beefcake?

local teen scrubber, was more than happy to let Jack get his shiny size tens under the table.

Max, on the other hand, wasn't quite so keen to discover Jack's new role and has been plotting his downfall ever since. Max has a gun, but what is he going to do with it? With Ronnie, Roxy, Tanya and Selina all notching up Jack's bedpost, no woman is safe with a man like Jack around. But be warned, ladies – the only person Jack will ever truly love is himself...

TOP OF THE LOTHARIO CHARTS. BUT AS JACK PUMPS HIS PECS IN HIS HOME-GYM, VARYING LEVELS OF LUCK...

Losers!

Garry
Poor old Gal's had little luck in the sack since his wife Lynne left him over four years ago. He was desperate to convince Dawn he was her knight in shining overalls, but she turned him down. Garry looks destined to stay a bachelor boy unless someone sweeps him off his feet very soon.

Ricky
He's never found getting a woman hard; it's holding on to them that Ricky struggles with. Sam, Bianca, Natalie, Melinda – they've all experienced life with Ricky, and all decided that they're better off without him. Funny that.

Minty
Flatmate Minty is equally as hopeless. After snaring Garry's mum Hazel, it all fell apart over her inability to stay in sunny Walford. He wed mate Heather as part of a wedding magazine scam, but we all knew it was never going to last.

Billy
Twice married, and once divorced, Billy's never going to make 'Husband Of The Year'. Replacing dippy Mo Slater for even dippier Honey Edwards seemed like the answer to his prayers. But changing wives doesn't mean he's changed his ways and after two years he's alone again. Third time lucky?

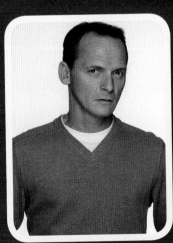

FISH-TICUFFS!

PRAWNY BIANCA JACKSON GIVES TROUTY JANE BEALE A BATTERING IN THE VIC AS THE RIVALROUS PAIR CLASH WHILE SERVING UP FISHY NIBBLES AT THE EAST LON-DON FISHMONGER'S BALL. STILL LOVIN' THOSE OUTFITS, LADIES!

Something fishy going on here...

Sea-feud!

Bianca puts Jane in her plaice...

Prawn to be wild!

Someone's getting crabby!

Who are you calling an old trout?

Keep starin' and I'll give you the fish finger!

Who called the carps?

(and that's enough fishy gags for one day...)

Sexy boy

WILL CALLUM MONKS BE LUCKIER
IN LOVE THAN DAD VINNIE?

From the minute Callum landed in Walford it was clear he was one of those boys that mums tell their daughters to keep away from – mostly because the mums want to get their mitts on him themselves! And that's just the way Callum likes it, because if charming the women of Walford were an Olympic sport he'd be the one on the podium with the gold medal and a smug face like the cat that got the cream.

The Square's latest hot young buck can turn his hands to most things, but unlike his hapless dad Vinnie, Callum's actually good at them. In the past he's had various bar jobs, been involved in the odd dosh-making scam and always had at least two or three women on the go at once. But while he may have been a ladies man, Callum had never actually had a proper girlfriend.

When he pitched up in E20 in August Callum decided that maybe it was time he rectified that situation – and on spotting a scantily clad Stacey struggling to unlock her front door, he was smitten. Of course this being Callum his knee-jerk reaction was to try and chat her up, whilst Stacey responded by doing her trademark scowly face thing in a bid to put him off. But even in that brief exchange there was no denying the instant attraction between them.

Meanwhile, Stacey agreed to try for a baby with dependable Bradley, but by September much as Stacey tried to resist Callum's charms the pair shared an intimate moment, which she immediately regretted and as a result guiltily threw herself into her relationship with Bradley.

However, Stacey started feeling pressurised by Bradley's baby-making plans and the ballsy market trader realised she had to make a difficult choice – Stacey Slater or Stacey Branning?

Whilst there's no denying Callum has enjoyed his first taste of going steady, there's no getting away from the fact that this is a guy who likes to share the love – how long will it be before he starts looking for the next notch on his bedpost?

> When Callum spotted a scantily clad Stacey his knee-jerk reaction was to chat her up

Callum looks set to break some Walford hearts

Yule love it!

OUR GUIDE TO A PERFECT COCKNEY CHRISTMAS KNEES-UP...

Ian's quick & easy mince pies

Ingredients
375g pack ready-rolled puff pastry
200g mincemeat
1 medium egg yolk, beaten with a little cold milk

Directions:

1. Preheat the oven to 200°C, Gas Mark 6. Unroll the pastry and flatten down on the work surface. Using shaped cutters, cut out an assortment of shapes, such as hearts, diamonds and stars, and place on 2 baking trays, spaced well apart.
2. Lightly prick the centre of each pastry shape with a fork. Brush with the egg and milk glaze.
3. Place a little mincemeat in the centre of each pastry shape and bake for 12–15 minutes or until risen and golden brown. Then allow to cool for a few minutes.

Ian's top tip: For a different vibe add rolled-up balls of marzipan on the pastry, then add the mincemeat and bake!

Mmmm...

Crimbo cocktails!

Snowball

Don't diss Nana Pat's favourite traditional Christmas drink – it's tastier than Jack Branning!

Boozy!

Directions:
A smooth blend of advocaat and lemonade with a dash of lime juice. Shake the advocaat and lime juice together. Pour into a big, ice-filled glass and top up with lemonade.

Fruity!

Merry Berry

Phil Mitchell's number one tipple – a fruity, festive, non-alcoholic cocktail to enjoy with family and friends.

Directions:
Mix together 75ml of orange juice with the same quantity of cranberry. Add tonic water to taste, stir well and garnish with a wedge of lime.

I bought all these presents for myself!

❄ Festive Do's & Don'ts

Do...

Declare your undying love! On Christmas Day 2003 Kat and Alfie Moon finally tied the knot – despite the fact that he was, erm, sort of already married. A true romantic, Alfie hired a snow machine that turned the Square into a winter wonderland.

Do...

Plan your Christmas shopping! Last year well-thought out gifts included Shirley giving Heather a vibrating 'slimming' machine, Heather giving Shirl a greased-up muscle man calendar and Dawn picking the perfect pressie for fetid step-dad Keith: a nose-hair trimmer.

Do...

Bring new life into the world! Liam Butcher was born in the Vic on Christmas Day ten years ago. Bianca's screams as arch-rival Grant assisted still ring in the ears of those who were there.

Don't...

Forget to defrost the turkey! When Mo panicked in 2005 that the Slaters' frozen turkey wouldn't defrost in time, she decided to get another bird from one of her dodgy mates. However, when the bird turned up it turned out to be Corky the Parrot!

Don't...

Play practical jokes! Okay, the whoopee cushion under Stella was well deserved, but the smoke pellet

TOP FIVE MOST MISERABLE FESTIVE MOMENTS... EVER!

FORGET THE SEASON OF GOODWILL – DOWN WALFORD WAY CHRISTMAS IS GUARANTEED TO END IN TEARS... OR DEATH

2001

Evil Trevor pours gravy onto Little Mo's Christmas dinner plate, pushes her face into it and then forces her to eat the turkey off the floor. On New Year's Eve Mo fights back and attacks Trevor about the head with an iron.

2002

Accident-prone Martin Fowler runs over Jamie Mitchell, who then dies on Christmas Day of spleen damage. As he lies on his deathbed Sonia pledges to love Jamie forever – 18 months later she marries Martin.

Queen Vic karaoke songlist

Bradley: 'Last Christmas'
Actually, maybe one to be avoided by Bradders. Who wants to be reminded about the day you found out your dad was having it away with your missus? Bleeeugh!

Patrick: 'Rockin' Around The Christmas Tree'
The trilby-hatted groover was once in his own band called The Five Hectors – who better to get this Crimbo party started?

Roxy: 'Santa Baby'
Roxy's Sexy Santa outfit was the best gift the male population of Walford could've asked for – a red-faced Ian Beale just couldn't take his eyes off her baubles.

Stacey: 'I Wish It Could Be Christmas Every Day'
Not when it involves a whack round the chops from Tanya Branning she doesn't!

in the Vic chimney maybe wasn't Ben's best idea. Peggy ordered Garry and Minty to investigate before poor Minty promptly fell off a ladder and injured himself.

Don't...
Get arrested! When Tiffany Mitchell fell down the stairs and was hospitalised with a blood clot, everyone assumed apeman Grant had pushed her – he spent his Yule behind bars, but for once he was innocent.

WHY DID THE TURKEY CROSS THE ROAD?

Because he wasn't chicken

WHO HIDES IN THE BAKERY AT CHRISTMAS?

A mince spy

2005
The good news: on Christmas Day Sharon thinks she has food poisoning but it turns out that, against the odds, she's pregnant. The bad news: hubby Dennis is stabbed days later and dies in Shazza's arms as the clock strikes midnight on New Year's Eve.

2006
A bitter and lonely Pauline Fowler keels over in the falling snow and corks it in the middle of the Square, having been slapped by arch enemy Sonia.

2007
The Brannings have a Christmas from hell. Highlights include Bradley punching Max, Bradley throwing up, Tanya slapping Max, Tanya slapping Stacey, Tanya throwing Max out and Bradley chucking Stacey out before sobbing uncontrollably to himself. Oh happy day!

Who's the boss?

WALFORD MAY BE A PLACE WHERE FAMILY COMES FIRST, BUT HOW WOULD ITS RESIDENT BROTHERS AND SISTERS FARE IN A BATTLE FOR SUPREMACY?

Ronnie v Roxy

TOUGH STUFF

Ronnie: Colder than an Arctic storm, it takes a lot to rile her. But when she blows, diving for cover from that right hook is advisable.

Roxy: While she'd rather avoid confrontation Roxy can slap with the best of them, and the claws have been known to come out, especially after a drink or two.

SEX APPEAL

Ronnie: Blonde hair and an impressive cleavage mean she's never short of male attention, and her unreachable, ice-maiden manner makes her irresistible to men who like a challenge.

Roxy: Why play hard to get when you're not? That's Roxy's motto. But despite her easy antics, still the men keep coming back for more. Even when pregnant, Roxy sizzled with sex appeal, but motherhood may mellow her.

MIND MATTERS

Ronnie: She could benefit from less thinking and more action. While she's definitely the more level-headed sister, her love of mind games – learned from dad Archie – hasn't always brought her happiness.

Roxy: She acts first and thinks later. But while she's not blessed with business nous, Roxy's no dumb blonde – she's smart enough to let Ronnie do all the hard work and get her out of trouble whenever necessary.

THE VERDICT

Life with Roxy is one big party, but if it's enigmatic and sultry you're after, Ronnie's (C) cup runneth over.

Max v Jack

TOUGH STUFF

Max: Max is a lover, not a fighter. His power lies in the spoken word, and if manipulation were a sport, Max would be an Olympic gold. Put him in a boxing ring, however, and he wouldn't last a round.

Jack: Ex-copper Jack certainly knows how to handle himself, and if his latest outbursts are anything to go by, one thing he didn't learn in the force was discipline. Definitely dangerous if crossed.

SEX APPEAL

Max: He may look a bit like a deflated space-hopper, but Max has never been short of admirers. A serial love rat, he had several extramarital flings – including daughter-in-law Stacey – before long-suffering Tanya finally kicked him out.

Jack: Jack has plenty of female fans. But unlike his brother, he doesn't go looking for lusty encounters – they find him. He bedded Roxy behind Ronnie's back and moved in with Tanya before Max had a chance to clear his sock drawer. Well, keeping it in the family is something of a tradition in Walford.

SIBLING RIVALRY!

MIND MATTERS

Max: As calculating as they come, Max can outmanoeuvre everyone, from his son Bradley to his long-suffering wives and mistresses, by pinpointing their weaknesses and going in for the kill.

Jack: It's becoming clear Jack didn't always play by the rules as a cop, but his past is yet to completely catch up with him, thanks to his clever covering of tracks. Max shouldn't underestimate him.

THE VERDICT

Max may have all the moves, but little brother Jack has had the connections, the looks and, most importantly, Tanya, making him the clear winner.

Jane v Christian

TOUGH STUFF

Jane: A lady who has had to handle herself with the likes of Peggy and Bianca in the past – as well as mud-wrestle Ian on her wedding day – it's safe to say Jane could take Christian in a fight.

Christian: While he's clearly at the peak of physical fitness, we imagine

smoothie Christian is more likely to diffuse disputes than resort to violence.

SEX APPEAL

Jane: Jane's womanly charms, no-nonsense manner and quiet determination has helped Ian banish the ghost of sultry Cindy and made her top of Grant's list for a holiday fling.

Christian: Only Pat can come close to Christian for bedpost notches and,

even with her stint as a prostitute thrown in, he'd probably still be a four-poster ahead.

MIND MATTERS

Jane: Smarter than the average Walford female, Jane is wasted in the café. But then, as business opportunities in the area go, it's on a par with a top job in Sir Alan Sugar's empire.

Christian: A master at seducing men and a confidant for women, Christian manages to ingratiate himself with who he wants, when he wants.

THE VERDICT

Domestic goddess Jane rules in the kitchen, but Christian has the charm – and better home furnishings.

Phil v Grant

TOUGH STUFF

Phil: While he's long been feared as Walford's resident thug, Phil's reputation means he's rarely challenged to a fight. Unless he's crossed or he's had a drink – at which point Phil's face turns an interesting shade of beetroot and heads are banged.

Grant: In the old days, ex-soldier Grant was by far the more volatile Mitchell, as his wives, the local cops and even his mum will testify, but

since moving abroad and becoming a dad, Grant has mellowed.

SEX APPEAL

Phil: He's pushing 50, yet still the women throw themselves at baldy Phil. Perhaps it's the heady mixture of Old Spice, engine oil and good old brutish charm.

Grant: Grant was never alone for long and married two of the Square's residents – Sharon and Tiffany – as well as Carla from Brazil. He proved he's still got it on his last trip back, when he seduced Jane. Although, considering her alternative was Ian, maybe she wasn't being that choosy...

MIND MATTERS

Phil: The brains of the outfit, Phil would much rather fit someone up or mess with their mind than get his hands dirty.

Grant: He fights. He charms. Sometimes he blubs. But Grant does not do quantum physics.

THE VERDICT

For sun, sea and a daily gut-buster breakfast, see Grant. If it's an iron fist and emotional baggage you're after, Phil's your man.

Sean v Stacey

TOUGH STUFF

Sean: He turned up in the Square after threatening to hang a former army mate from a tree and has kept up the hard-man image by duffing up Gus and Mickey, though they don't really count.

Stacey: While she's carried on Kat's good work as Walford's Resident Gobby Slater, Stacey's so far proved to be all mouth and no trousers – or should that be no knickers? She's traded insults with the best of them, but has thrown more drinks than punches.

SEX APPEAL

Sean: The women of Albert Square can't get enough of ginger ninja Sean, and with competition like Minty, Ian and Winston Off The Market, who can blame them?

Stacey: She may have been around the block, but the male population of Walford is not immune to Stacey's chavvy charms – most of them uttering 'you would' at some point.

MIND MATTERS

Sean: A dark place where few dare venture – that's Sean's brain. In the neurological department, it's safe to say he's busier conquering demons than doing Sudoku.

Stacey: Again, not exactly a deep thinker, but Stacey is definitely 'street smart'. Which, in Walford terms, means knowing how to lie convincingly, hide evidence of adultery and flog rank clothes at the market.

THE VERDICT

In terms of pure entertainment value, Sean provides plenty of fireworks, but Stacey's more likely to keep her head in a crisis. Or, indeed, any other situation.

One of the good guys

IS LUCAS JOHNSON A MAN TORMENTED BY HIS PAST?

When Denise Wicks arrived back from her travels to find her drugged-up daughter being comforted by her druggie ex she was understandably not best pleased. But once she'd got over her initial shock – and Chelsea had got over her brief drugs hell – Lucas managed to persuade Denise that he was a changed man and as a result there has been a softening of hostilities between the feisty matriarch and her former beau.

It was when his estranged daughter Chelsea decided to track

A furious Denise is reuinted with Lucas

Lucas hadn't made contact with Chelsea for fear of destroying her life

down and make contact with her dad that we got our first glimpse of Lucas Johnson. Much to Chelsea's dismay, it turned out the druggie father that had abandoned her when she was a child had turned his life around and was now a pastor at a chapel in Peckham. He was equally as stunned when Chelsea revealed herself to be his long-lost daughter – but she ran off in tears before he had the chance to say a word.

Two months later, Patrick invited Lucas to Chelsea's 22nd birthday party – but Chelsea gave him short shrift, until he explained what had happened in the past: that he was only 17 years old when Denise gave birth, too young to be a dad and he'd managed eventually

to overcome his drug habit and start again with a clean slate. He hadn't made contact with Chelsea for fear of destroying her life.

After talking to Patrick, Chelsea reluctantly agreed to give the charismatic preacher a second chance but the discovery that she had a half-brother – 12-year-old Jordan – was too much for her and she descended into a spiral of drug addiction. It was up to Lucas to save the day when he rescued a coked-up Chelsea from R&R, where she was surrounded by a braying gang of men.

In June, again much to Denise's displeasure, Lucas announced he'd paid a deposit on a flat in the Square, in order for him and happy-go-lucky son Jordan to be closer to Chelsea. Since putting down roots in E20, Lucas has set up a youth club at the community centre and is now happy to call Walford home. And while Denise is never going to be ecstatic about having this particularly good-looking ghost from the past on her doorstep – for the moment, at least, she's remembering the good times and tolerating him.

Lucas comforts a tearful Chelsea

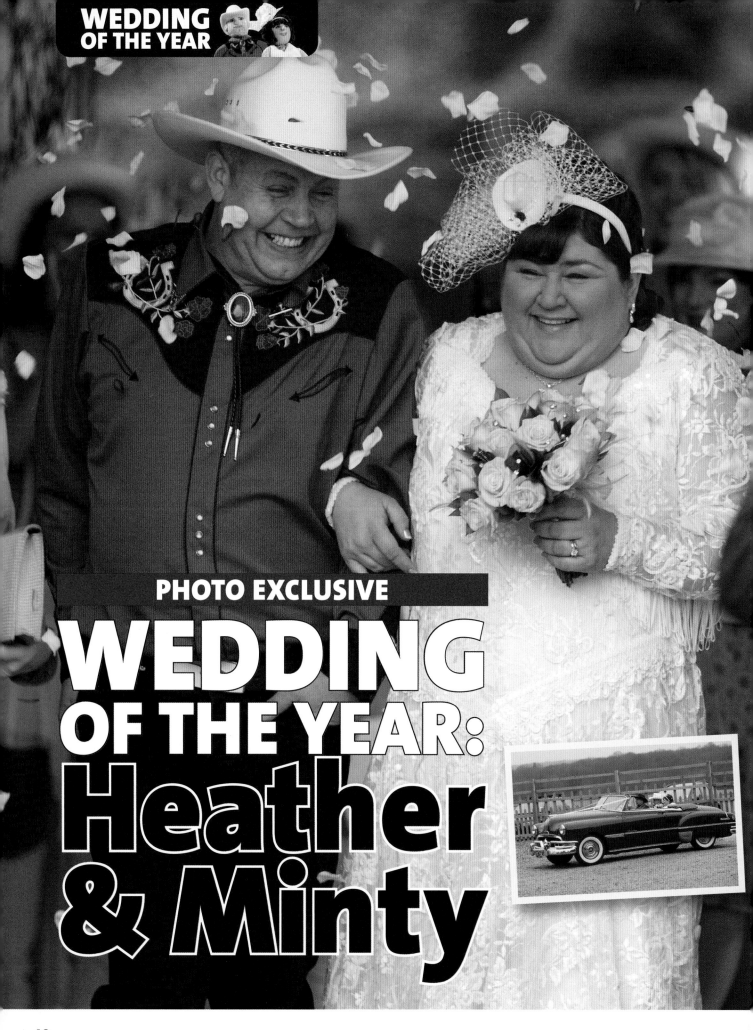

PHOTO EXCLUSIVE

WEDDING OF THE YEAR: Heather & Minty

IT STARTED OUT AS A MAGAZINE COMPETITION SCAM, BUT AS THE SUN SHONE ON WALFORD IN APRIL THIS YEAR, A LOVED-UP HEATHER TROTT AND MINTY PETERSON WERE EVENTUALLY MARRIED FOR REAL AT BARN HALL. OKAY, IT MAY HAVE ONLY LASTED AS LONG AS PARIS HILTON'S POP CAREER AND THEY NEVER ACTUALLY INDULGED IN ANY WEDDING NIGHT RUMPYPUMPY – BUT IT WAS STILL A DAY TO REMEMBER...

The ride of their lives?

All smiles: Mr and Mrs Peterson.

The happy couple after the ceremony

'Those girls at school. They used to say I'd end up on my own, stinking of cats in some high rise. But they were wrong. Cos I'm really doing it. I'm really getting married...'
Heather

49

The groom and best man Phil

Anyone fancy a bit of 'Agadoo'?

'I haven't been in the saddle since May Bank Holiday 2003'
Heather

The look of love: Hev and Minty

The 'mini me' bride and groom in marzipan

'No job, no home, no I just hope looking

HE RETURNED TO BURY HIS DAD BUT AFTER A FEW DAYS BACK IN WALFORD RICKY BUTCHER SOON REALISED THERE'S NO PLACE LIKE HOME...

Reunited in 2008

Curtains twitched around the Square as bumbling mechanic Ricky Butcher returned to Walford this year following his dad's death. If the neighbours hadn't spotted him leading the mourners at Frank's funeral, they were informed of his comeback thanks to the internationally recognised cry of 'Rickaaaaaay' by ex-wife Bianca a few days after.

The smell of the petrol-leaking Arches, the sound of Peggy throwing another punter out of the Vic, and the unforgettable vision of Dot Branning dragging on her 476th Lambert & Butler of the day – yes, Ricky was back where he belonged. Having spent 14 of the past 20 years in Walford, Ricky knows he'll never truly be able to stay away. After two failed marriages to Sam Mitchell and Bianca in the nineties, Ricky left the Square in 2000, only to return two years later.

A further two years on Albert Square ended in yet more misery after botched affairs with exes Sam and Natalie and the discovery that sister Janine was a cold-blooded killer. In 2004 it was time to discover whether the common denominator in all his unhappiness was Walford, and off he went. It wasn't.

Even without living life in the shadow of stepmum Pat's giant pineapple earrings, Ricky found that he was just no good at that thing called love, having fallen for gold-digging bimbo Melinda. After she discovered that he'd only inherited a rusty toolbox from his late dad Frank, Melinda dropped poor Ricky, leaving him without a job or a home, which led to his third return to Albert Square. It seemed to him that Queen Victoria and unfailingly affectionate Pat were the only two women never to let Ricky down, and with the vague hope of a reunion with true love Bianca in the pipeline, the slow-witted single dad reluctantly pitched up at his old stomping ground.

It didn't take the Butcher heir long to find his feet, joining his dad's ex-wife for the revival of Pat's cab service, and pledging unrelenting devotion to Bianca, despite her distinct apathy towards him. With Frank now dearly departed, it's up to Ricky to carry on the family name in the neighbourhood – if only he could replicate some of his dad's luck with women while he does it...

SEE MORE RICKY SNAPS OVER THE PAGE...

'no money, relationship. my dad ain't down on me!'

Look Who's Back!

RICKY BUTCHER: LOVED AND LOST

Cute! Floppy haired and fresh faced in 1988

After all their affairs and infidelities Ricky and Bianca finally tie the knot in April 1997

A child is born – Liam arrives on Christmas Day, 1998

Bianca's best mate Natalie snares Ricky for herself in 1995 and 2003

For old times sake? Ricky beds first-wife Sam Mitchell in 2003

Unlucky in love yet again – fiancée Melinda dumps a skint Ricky in 2008

WALFORD
TOTTY
Shabnam
Masood

55

The Gold digger

HAS PHIL FINALLY
MET HIS MATCH IN
SUZY BRANNING?

at the Vic, where Suzy thanked him the only way she knew – in bed. The following day the money-grabbing minx sneaked straight back to the salon for her precious bar of gold.

A month later Suzy reappeared in Walford to lie low, staying with stepmother Dot when she discovered her brothers were in no position to put her up. Actually, both Jack and Max seem generally irri-

A perfect match? Suzy and Phil

At first glance you wouldn't think Suzy was a Branning. She doesn't come across as tough-nosed as Max, Jack and Carol and in her designer shoes, spray tan and immaculate nails she initially seemed more concerned with not letting her shiny pink handbag out of her sight, than having a brawl in the street like the rest of her clan.

However it soon became clear that under that fluffy exterior Suzy was as hard as nails and had the trademark Branning shard of ice running through her. It turned out

Suzy thanked him the only way she knew how – in bed

the only reason she was so obsessed with the whereabouts of her girly pink handbag was not because it contained an expensive lip-gloss, but a hugely valuable lump of gold she'd just stolen from her ex.

It was in July that Max asked Phil Mitchell to deliver some cash to his older sister who was apparently in some kind of trouble. Phil found Suzy in Tantasy – the salon were she worked – and as is often the way with a male Mitchell, ended up punching some heavies before whisking her back to safety

Trouble for Suzy in Tantasy

tated by their sassy sister. However with all the dramas going on in his life Max needed some support and Suzy proved to be a useful ally when she moved him into her new home at the renovated Miller house.

Phil and Suzy picked up were they left off – with Suzy lovin' Phil's powerful streak and, of course, his money. Meanwhile Phil was put off getting into anything too heavy after what happened last year with his loony-tune ex-fiancée, Stella. But Phil's no fool – he knows sexy Suzy looks good on his arm and he can't get enough of the way she massages his ego, amongst other things. It doesn't happen very often in Walford but for once here's a pairing that look like they were well and truly made for each other!

'You should've let me know Frank. I'd have held your hand...'
– Pat

R.I.P.
Francis 'Frank' Aloysius BUTCHER
27 March 1940 to 29 March 2008

ORDER OF SERVICE

Francis Aloysius Butcher

27th March 1940 - 29th March 2008

A wreath poignantly spelt out his name as Walford bade a sad farewell to one of its favourite sons – the unforgettable Frank Butcher. But of course this was not the first time Frank had died as ex-wife Peggy was only too happy to point out. Six years ago she travelled to Spain after hearing Frank had been killed in a car crash and was understandably slightly taken aback to find him alive and well and attending his own funeral. It turned out he had faked his death in order to pull off a timeshare property scam.

But this time it was for real and with the Butcher clan gathered in the Square to say a final goodbye, Frank's death hit Pat – undoubtedly the love of his life – the hardest. Distraught at not having had the chance to say goodbye, Pat could only take comfort from the gifts her childhood sweetheart had left her on his deathbed – the revolving bow tie he wore naked on her doorstep and a picture of their wedding day (a full-on Cockney street party in the summer of 1989) with a note saying: 'The happiest day of my life.'

But when it came to less happy days, the forever duckin' 'n divin' charmer probably had more to choose from. First there was the time he torched the car lot as part of an insurance con, inadvertently killing a tramp who'd been dossing there, but probably top of his list of not-so-great moments would have to be the time he mowed down Tiffany Mitchell in his Jag outside the Vic. Whatever the locals may have thought of him, life was never predictable when Frank Butcher was around.

Before his death that occured whilst living in Manchester, Frank's dying wish was for his ashes to be scattered in the gardens of the square he loved, surrounded by the people he loved. A true East Ender to the very end – in death Frank Butcher had finally come home. ⟫→

Back in Walford to pay their respects: Diane, Pat, Ricky and Janine

R.I.P.
Jason 'Jase' DYER

Died: 25 August 2008

With a past he'd rather forget about, it was a fresh start that Jase Dyer wanted when he moved to Walford. But Jase's gangland years soon came back to haunt him and ultimately led to his tragic and untimely death.

After a period in the nick, the estranged father turned up in Albert Square in 2007 in search of his tearaway son Jay – so imagine his joy when his first glimpse of his long, lost sprog was of him cockily mooning at his granddad, Bert.

Keeping Jay on the straight and narrow proved to be a full-time job for the softly spoken ex-con, but he still found time to strip off to his boxer shorts in the launderette, causing Honey Mitchell to look even more wide-eyed and owl-like than usual.

He then dated the hottest babes in Walford and after a fling with Roxy Mitchell, he got together with Dawn

Swann and proposed.

But it was the handsome carpenter's disturbing relationship with his nemesis, Terry Bates – the gang boss who'd looked after him as a teen – that was to be his downfall. Terry and his hitmen had already tried to kill Jase once by storming the Vic but had only managed to hospitalise a pregnant Honey in the process.

However, on the night before their wedding and as Dawn celebrated her low-key hen night, he was tracked down and attacked by Terry who wanted revenge for Jase leaving the old firm. With a bereft Dawn left heartbroken by their stolen future and angry son Jay out for revenge, Jase Dyer may be gone, but he's not forgotten...

Above: Rest in Peace, Jase
Left: With fiancée Dawn in happier times

In mourning: a tearful Abi buried Marge in the backyard

R.I.P. MARGE the Guinea Pig

Died: 13 March 2008

After a short illness, Marge passed away at Booty – Tanya Branning had taken the under-the-weather guinea pig there to keep an eye on her. She was found dead in her cage shortly after a visit to the salon by loony-tune Sean, but despite initial suspicions, there is no evidence to prove that Psycho Slater strangled the much-loved pig. After a tearful burial by Abi in the front yard of No. 5, Marge was quickly replaced – but not forgotten – by Gilbert The Chinchilla.

R.I.P. WELLARD

Died: 15 August 2008

Walford's most well-known mutt has been involved in more dramas than some of its human residents. Much loved by Robbie Jackson, Gus and finally Bianca's rowdy brood, he's survived a bus crash, been kidnapped and even 'arrested' for biting Ian Beale's backside, which resulted in the 'WOOF' campaign: 'Walford One Owed Freedom'. The aged pooch was put down in August this year

No more woofing: Liam says goodbye to Wellard

after becoming seriously ill, with his post-mortem revealing it was all the chocolate in his stomach that had finished him off. A tearful Tiffany insisted Wellard deserved his own proper funeral – and after 14 years in the Square we agreed. It was time to say goodbye to a Walford legend...

Quiz of the Year

SO HAVE YOU BEEN PAYING ATTENTION FOR THE LAST 12 MONTHS? TRY OUR FUN QUIZ AND FIND OUT IF YOU'RE A WHIZZ ON WALFORD...

1. Where were Bianca and her brood (above) forced to spend the night before returning to Walford?
- [ ] (a) A bus shelter
- [ ] (b) A park
- [ ] (c) A shop doorway

2. What is the name of Jack Branning's daughter who came to visit this year?
- [ ] (a) Pippa
- [ ] (b) Penny
- [ ] (c) Peaches

3. Which Walford favourite returned to the Square this year to celebrate their birthday?
- [ ] (a) Grant Mitchell
- [ ] (b) Pauline Fowler
- [ ] (c) Jim Branning

4. Lucy threatened to run away again if she wasn't allowed to live with...
- [ ] (a) Pat
- [ ] (b) Christian
- [ ] (c) Lauren

5. Minty and Hazel/Heather (above) won a wedding competition in which magazine?
- ☐ (a) To Love And To Cherish
- ☐ (b) Till Death Do Us Part
- ☐ (c) Ball & Chain

6. What is the name of the former Walford medic who returned this year and blew up the Miller house?
- ☐ (a) Bonkers Brenda
- ☐ (b) Mad May
- ☐ (c) Loony Louise

7. At which seaside resort was a smitten Peggy reunited with brother-in-law Archie?
- ☐ (a) Southend
- ☐ (b) Leigh On Sea
- ☐ (c) Weymouth

8. Who tried to pay newly-arrived heartthrob Callum to leave Albert Square?
- ☐ (a) Phil Mitchell
- ☐ (b) Max Branning
- ☐ (c) Jean Slater

9. Which *Star Wars* film character did Clare Bates dress up as for Bradley?
- ☐ (a) Princess Leia
- ☐ (b) Darth Vader
- ☐ (c) Jabba The Hutt

10. What was the reason for the flood at the Masoods'?
- ☐ (a) Shabnam left the bath running
- ☐ (b) A burst pipe
- ☐ (c) Freak weather conditions

11. Who organised the Best Of British Day – which saw Ian Beale being pelted with wet sponges in the stocks?
- ☐ (a) Shirley
- ☐ (b) Phil
- ☐ (c) Ronnie

12. What is preacher Lucas Johnson's relationship with Chelsea Fox?
- ☐ (a) Stepfather
- ☐ (b) Father
- ☐ (c) Long-lost uncle

13. What is the name of the catering business Ian and brother-in-law Christian decided to open together?
- ☐ (a) Fit For A Queen
- ☐ (b) Mine's A Large One
- ☐ (c) Munch On That

14. Who won the highly contended barmaid of the year competition (above)?
- ☐ (a) Dawn
- ☐ (b) Roxy
- ☐ (c) Peggy

≫⟶

15. Why did Honey Mitchell leave Billy, taking their
children with her (left)?
- [ ] *(a) He was having an affair*
- [ ] *(b) Because of his involvement in Jase's death*
- [ ] *(c) Billy was a bigamist*

16. What is the name of the gang boss who killed Jase?
- [ ] *(a) Toby Brown*
- [ ] *(b) Tim Boyd*
- [ ] *(c) Terry Bates*

17. What did Frank Butcher leave his money-grabbing
daughter Janine in his will?
- [ ] *(a) A property in Spain*
- [ ] *(b) Family jewellery*
- [ ] *(c) Her grandmother's diary*

Who said What?

WHEN IT COMES TO TELLING IT LIKE IT IS NO-ONE DOES IT BETTER THAN THE RESIDENTS OF E20. BUT WHO OFFERED UP THESE GEMS?

1. *'No-one calls my daughter stupid except me – alright!'*

2. *'Every time I open the cupboard I think Chucky's gonna jump out and attack me with a meat cleaver!'*

3. *'I give the orders around here, not that great big lump of lard.'*

4. *'I'm gonna tell Tanya what you're really like. Then maybe she can throw you back in the gutter where you belong.'*

5. *'I've got to learn to let go – I can't control everything. Least of all what my little sister does.'*

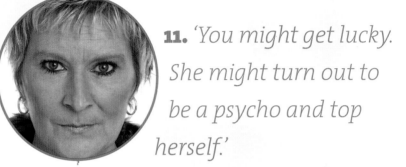

6. *'Last week you needed stabilisers – this week you're like a dog on heat.'*

7. *'Good guys only win in movies – I can't believe you haven't learnt that yet.'*

8. *'Punters who spend less time ogling you might spend more on beer.'*

9. *'You are the Kenny to my Dolly. Things just don't feel right without you.'*

10. *'All he ever wanted from you was sex. You kept him in the Square like a fly in your web til you were ready for him.'*

11. *'You might get lucky. She might turn out to be a psycho and top herself.'*

12. *'You and me are going to form our own club – the everyone hates us but we don't care club.'*

13. *'I'd like to thank you, Shirley. I think you've taught us a lot. Like what happens if you don't slap on enough sun-block while you're young.'*

Bad Girl

AFTER HER EVIL PLOTTING WAS EXPOSED, CLARE BATES' RETURN WAS TO END IN TEARS.

utter wouldn't have melted in Clare's mouth when she first appeared in Walford as a sweet, ponytailed eight-year-old schoolgirl. However, ten years later who could've predicted she'd return as a fishnet-wearing uber-bitch whose cruel skulduggery would give even the likes of Janine a run for her dubiously earned money.

Not that fresh-faced Clare didn't have moments of bitchery even then – she spread rumours that elderly local barber Felix was a pervert who had murdered his wife and kept her mutilated body in his cellar and then inflicted a major bullying campaign on her supposed best friend Sonia Jackson. Well, all that trumpet-playing would get on anyone's nerves in the end...

But by this stage Clare had been through the mill. Her mum Debbie had been killed in a hit and run road accident and she became the focus of a bitter custody battle between her violent dad Liam and loveable stepfather Nigel Bates. When Nigel won, it looked like this was a happy ending for Clare as she left to start a new life in Scotland with Nigel, his new girlfriend Julie and her rather dishy son, Josh.

A family portrait from 1993

Clare's tried everything short of whipping her clothes off and doing the hokey-cokey on Arthur's bench to nab a bloke

But it seems the decade since we last saw Clare hadn't gone quite so swimmingly and she arrived back in Walford with a bump in February when she was chucked out of a moving car by her sugar daddy ex-lover. Homeless and penniless, she was taken in by stepfather Nigel's former landlady Dot and soon got work at Booty, leaving co-worker Chelsea in no doubt that Clare was a woman with an evil streak.

But it was Walford's men that Clare saw as her money ticket and she tried everything short of whipping her clothes

off and doing the hokey-cokey on Arthur's bench in order to nab one. She dressed up as Princess Leia to snare Bradley and Ian Beale was completely beguiled by her, but she only had eyes for his wallet and blackmailed him.

Ironically, it was the men of Walford that proved to be Clare's downfall and she was exposed as a manipulative seductress when her little black book was discovered by Bradley and Stacey. Whilst Dot tried to support her as she faced up to her demons, in August Clare's hard facade finally crumbled as Bradley told her exactly what he thought of her and she quit E20 for good. See you in another ten years then, Clare!

Clare's manhunt continues on 'Singles' Night'

Clare and her little black book in 2008

How To Be A Complete Bitch by Clare Bates

1. Lie & cheat – spin it so you win it
2. Steal – well, if Dot will leave her purse lying around...
3. Show maximum cleavage at all times – v. important!

CRIMES OF FASHION

WHEN IT COMES TO A BAD CLOTHES' DAY, WALFORD RESIDENTS ARE THE PEARLY KINGS AND QUEENS OF FASHION FAUX-PAS. HERE ARE THOSE LOCALS WHO GOT DRESSED IN THE DARK THIS YEAR...

Walford's answer to Carrie Bradshaw pulls off yet another shocker!

Slashed sleeves and sequins, Shirl? We're seeing red!

Clare shows us her wares – very down (Bridge Street) market

Oh, Bianca. It's not 1993 – time to ditch the Puffa...

Curry on a sleeve? It's all the rage on the catwalks of Milan this season!

Heather does her best Frank Butcher impression

We're not sure what's scarier – the glare on Pat's face or the glare from this electricity-conducting cape?

Lovin' those earrings!

Green, amber – how about red for stop? Libby comes dressed as a traffic light

Did Trinny and Susannah spontaneously vomit over Shirley when they saw this monstrosity?

Honey, luv – the Easter Bunny wants its coat back!

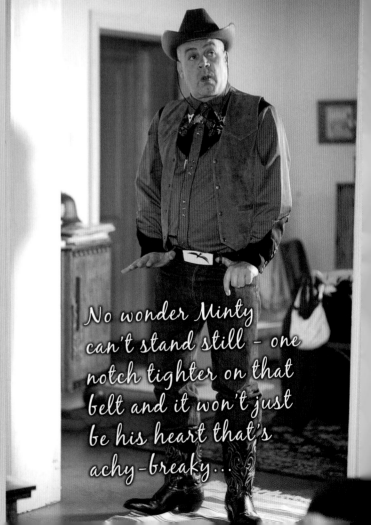

No wonder Minty can't stand still – one notch tighter on that belt and it won't just be his heart that's achy-breaky...

Mo's t-shirt is smiling but we're not laughing!

Oh, Bradley, what have you come as – a tub of Neapolitan?

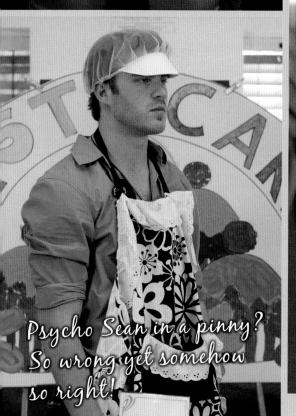

Psycho Sean in a pinny? So wrong yet somehow so right!

The Rihanna bob doesn't quite work for Chelsea!

A to Z of EastEnders

D is for Doctor Who
Bradley is almost as obsessed with The Doctor as he is with James Bond. When estranged wife Stacey bought him tickets for a Doctor Who convention it looked like the couple were going to be reunited – but surrounded by Daleks and Cybermen, Bradley merely gave a tearful Stacey an envelope containing his wedding ring and told her it was over.

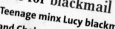

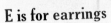

E is for earrings
Pat Evans' ginormous earrings are as much a fixture of Albert Square as the Queen Vic itself. But not everyone is a fan. After deciding to give his cheating wife Pat another chance after her affair with Frank, hubby Roy decided to tell some home truths with the shock revelation that he'd never liked her earrings and found them cheap and tacky. Tacky? Surely not.

A is for Arthur's bench
The dedication on the plaque reads: 'In Memory Of Arthur Fowler. He Loved It Here.' Probably because it was somewhere to escape from the clutches of his hatchet-faced wife Pauline. Many a relationship has ended and many a future has been contemplated on this mossy seat. No doubt Wellard has relieved himself on it a few times as well.

B is for blackmail
Teenage minx Lucy blackmailed Deano and Chelsea, Claire blackmailed Ian as did Janine after Ian began to use her 'special massage' services. And if ever there's a cautionary tale about blackmail, it's Janine's – when Ian's wife Laura found out what was going on she threw a pan of boiling milk in Janine's face, which caused Janine to become agoraphobic and start eating dog food.

C is for Cindy
Ian's nightmare began when Lucy was contacted by someone on the internet claiming to be her long-dead mother, Cindy. Soon this nutter was waging a campaign of terror against a gibbering Ian, who was then held hostage for three weeks in a deserted block of flats. Was it really Cindy back from the dead? No, it was her mad-eyed, gun-toting son Steven who'd totally lost the plot.

F is for friendship
Garry and Minty, Heather and Shirley, Peggy and Pat. Here are three Walford best friendships that have stood the test of time despite the fact they are falling out as often as they're getting on.

G is for goodbye

Unlucky in love street-sweeper Gus waved goodbye to the Square in May to go on tour with new girlfriend Keisha. After failed romances with the likes of Sonia Jackson, the gentle poet deserves a bit of happiness, as well as a Blue Peter badge for lasting as long as he did flat-sharing with an increasingly deranged Sean Slater.

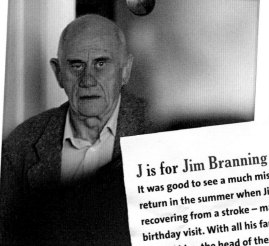

J is for Jim Branning

It was good to see a much missed face return in the summer when Jim – recovering from a stroke – made a birthday visit. With all his family around him, the head of the Branning clan couldn't have been happier. But when evil Max tried to build bridges, his father made it very clear his eldest son wasn't welcome. You tell him, Jimbo!

H is for heartache

That's what Lucy caused Jane and Ian this year when she disappeared for months on end. As the family desperately tried to find her, it turned out that loon Steven knew where she was all along. Ian begged bratty Lucy to come home and she agreed, but only on the condition that if she didn't get her own way in the future she'd leave again. Charming!

K is for kids

The kids of Walford can be a troublesome lot – from Jay terrorising Dot to Whitney stealing from Stacey's stall, there's always someone up to no good. Except for Tamwar Masood who is never happier than when immersed in a text book or researching something fascinating about Pythagorus on the internet. We give him a year or so before he goes bad like the rest of them.

I is for internet
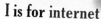

You had to admire Darren and Libby's online entrepreneurial skills. First of all they pretended to be Mickey's girlfriend Li Chong and uploaded pictures of her onto their website www.desperaterussianhousewives.co.uk, before hiding webcams around No 27 to spy on bath-shy dad Keith for another of their internet ideas – the inspired www.watchagrownmanrot.co.uk.

M is for mums

What would life in Walford be like without its matriarchs? From Peggy Mitchell to Denise Wicks, Zainab Masood to Pat Evans – their families would be lost without their mothers to hold it all together. Although probably the scariest of them all is Heather's battle-axe 'Mummy' Queenie Trott. A woman so sour-faced she makes the late, great Pauline Fowler look positively smiley.

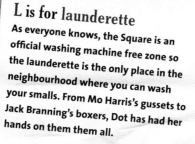

L is for launderette

As everyone knows, the Square is an official washing machine free zone so the launderette is the only place in the neighbourhood where you can wash your smalls. From Mo Harris's gussets to Jack Branning's boxers, Dot has had her hands on them them all.

R is for R&R!

The club co-owned by on-off lovebirds Jack Branning and Ronnie Mitchell has been the scene of many a drunken night out. Previously known as Scarlet, the E20 and, perhaps most unlikely of all, Angie's Den.

N is for nappies

The births of Oscar Branning, Summer Swann and William Mitchell mean the Minute Mart needs to be well stocked with baby basics. Next to be up to her neck in rancid nappies and kiddy poo is Roxy — now this we cannot wait to see!

Q is for the Queen Vic

The very heart of Albert Square and the perfect place for a cockney knees up or just somewhere to drown your sorrows. Liam Butcher was born in the Vic on Christmas Day in 1998 and in 2005 dodgy Den Watts was buried in the pub's cellar by his murdering wife Chrissie. Read more about life at the Vic in our special feature on page 114.

S is for sick

Which is how Gus felt when he thought psycho Sean had used his beloved Wellard as the meat filling in his spag bol. So much so he even ended up vomiting all over Dawn's best dress during her barmaid competition photoshoot. Thankfully for everyone concerned, it turned out our four-legged hero was alive and well.

O is for out & proud

At last Walford has a big gay who isn't all angsty about his sexuality. R&R barman Christian Clarke is out and proud and we love him for that. Even an initially panicked Ian Beale seems to be warming to Albert Square's romeo dancing queen.

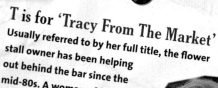

T is for 'Tracy From The Market'

Usually referred to by her full title, the flower stall owner has been helping out behind the bar since the mid-80s. A woman of few words, she seems to mainly communicate by nodding. When Dennis Rickman first arrived in Albert Square they had a one-night stand — this was revealed when he returned her knickers to her over the bar. Needless to say, Tracy had little to say on the subject.

P is for punch

Or should that be right hook? She may come across as a composed ice queen, but when Ronnie Mitchell whacked Sean Slater to the ground with her fist she proved she was Walford's answer to Amir Khan (in a blonde wig).

U is for unfinished business

When an unhinged Dr May reappeared on the scene this year it could only mean one thing – big trouble for Dawn and The Millers. But even they couldn't have predicted that the mad medic would blow up their house with Dawn and Mickey inside. Talk about going out with a bang!

X is for x-rated

There have been quite a few glimpses of pasty male flesh around these parts – whether it was Bradley naked but for a well-placed bottle of Asti to spare his blushes, Sean shower-fresh in just a towel or, less successfully, poor virginal Steven butt naked on the bed ready for Stacey only to be given the once over by a smirking Christian instead. Let's hear it for the boys!

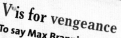

V is for vengeance

To say Max Branning wasn't exactly chuffed when he found out his brother Jack was having it away with his estranged wife Tanya would be something of an understatement. Frothing at the mouth in utter fury might be a better way to describe it. Intent on getting revenge, Mad Max enlisted Phil to help frame Jack and attempted to get him sent daaaaan.

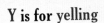

Y is for yelling

There's a lot of yelling and shouting that goes on down Walford way – from the inevitable 'Gerrouta my pub!' to the ear-bashing 'Rickaaaaaaaaaaaaay!' The quietest man there has to be Whispering Phil Mitchell – someone who talks so quietly only bats can hear him.

Z is for Zainab Masood

It took a woman of strength and courage to spend a night at the Millers' flea pit, but desperate times called for desperate measures when Chez Masood was flooded. It was so filthy she ended up bedding down on the floor of the Post Office for one night before scrubbing the Millers' gaff from top to bottom. Mama Masood even gave Keith's rim the once over. That woman deserves a medal!

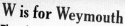

W is for Weymouth

There's nothing the townies of Walford love more than a trip to the seaside. This year was no different as Peggy and Ronnie headed to Dorset to bring Roxy back to the Square. The long-lost relative was their manipulative dad Archie who fought with Ronnie for control of pregnant Roxy – who spent most of her time tearfully swigging vodka on a revolving fairground ride!

Who's that girl?

A NEW FRIEND FOR STACEY
WANTS TO MAKE HER FORTUNE

Like Dick Whittington, Danielle came to London to seek her fortune and hoped the big smoke would have more to offer than life back in her home town of Telford – quite a big step for someone who doesn't exactly come across as Little Miss Confident.

As a child Danielle was always the girl on the edge of the crowd. She did averagely well at school but one thing she found she was good at was drama. She scooped the role of Jan in a school production of Grease and despite the fact that gawky Jan was perhaps the least interesting of the Pink Ladies, for once this shy, slightly needy teenager was really enjoying herself.

Danielle arrived on the Square in August and soon found herself a job on Stacey's market stall. She wasn't a natural barrow girl but gradually picked up tips from gobsters Stacey and Mo, whilst simultaneously developing a blush-inducing crush on Mr Fruit & Veg himself, Callum Monks.

Facing the future: Danielle arrived in E20 in August

As a little girl, no matter how hard she tried, Danielle never did quite fit in

To supplement her income so she could afford to pay the train fare to visit her family in Shropshire, the hardworking teen also bagged cleaning jobs at both The Vic and R&R.

However it was the Slaters who really took Danielle under their wing – Charlie, Mo and Jean liked having her around and when her mate Stacey moved in with Bradley, Danielle ended up renting her old room. More than anything else Danielle was chuffed she was made to feel like an honorary member of this close-knit clan, because as a little girl growing up in Shropshire, no matter how hard she tried, she never did quite fit in.

Who ♥ is your perfect EastEnders date?

TAKE OUR PROBING AND PSYCHOLOGICAL QUIZ AND FIND OUT WHICH WALFORD
RESIDENT IS THE ONE FOR YOU...

1. In an ideal world what would you choose to do on your perfect first date?

- [ ] a) A candlelit dinner for two
- [ ] b) A night at the flicks
- [ ] c) A few cans of extra strong lager followed by a curry
- [ ] d) A nice bit of rumpy-pumpy

2. Which of the following films would you choose to watch on a date?

- [ ] a) *Knocked Up*
- [ ] b) *Quantum Of Solace*
- [ ] c) *Seed of Chucky*
- [ ] d) *The Italian Job*

3. You pick your date up at their house. They answer the door. The first words you say are:

- [ ] a) 'I want to undress you right now.'
- [ ] b) 'You look lovely!'
- [ ] c) 'You're not leaving the house looking like that?'
- [ ] d) 'Can I use your khazi? My bladder's about to explode...'

4. Do you think the main topic of first-date conversation should be:

- [ ] a) flirtatious and light-hearted
- [ ] b) intellectually stimulating
- [ ] c) drunken and full of attitude
- [ ] d) all about your date trying to sell you a dodgy knock-off watch

5. An embarrassing pause in the conversation occurs during your date. As tumbleweed drifts across the table, do you:

- [ ] a) Say nothing. It will take care of itself
- [ ] b) Pretend you've just received a text message
- [ ] c) Yawn with boredom
- [ ] d) Tell a joke

6. The bill arrives. Do you:

- [ ] a) Grab it and insist on paying it yourself
- [ ] b) Reach for it and suggest splitting the bill
- [ ] c) Ignore it and hope your date picks up the tab
- [ ] d) Do a runner

7. The bill is paid and the night is full of possibilities. Do you:

- [ ] a) Say: 'Wanna go clubbing? I know just the place and I reckon I can get us on the guest list.'
- [ ] b) Ask your date if they want some chewing gum or a minty lozenge
- [ ] c) Wink suggestively and say: 'Your place or mine?'
- [ ] d) Slip the tip into your pocket when no-one is looking

8. As you're walking out of the restaurant you both see a £50 note on the floor. Do you:

- [ ] a) Slip it silently into the waiter's hand - he or she gave great service and deserves it
- [ ] b) Hand it in to the manager, telling them someone must have dropped it
- [ ] c) Check the coast is clear and stuff it in your pocket without saying a word
- [ ] d) Elbow your date out of the way as you jump on it yelling: 'Gerroff - I saw it first!'

Your perfect date is...

Mostly A's
Charming and Confident! You know what you want and you know just how to achieve it

Your Dream Date:
Jack Branning

Mostly B's
Polite and Thoughtful! You put others first – but sometimes you're a bit too eager to please

Your Dream Date:
Bradley Branning

Mostly C's
Boozy and Unpredictable! You like to make your dates work hard – and play hard

Your Dream Date:
Shirley Carter

Mostly D's
Gobby and Gagging For It! You don't suffer fools gladly – unless they are paying the bill

Your Dream Date:
Mo Harris

Dear Pat...

OUR AGONY AUNT **PAT EVANS** HAS BEEN THERE, DONE IT AND BOUGHT THE NOVELTY EARRINGS. SO WHO BETTER TO SORT OUT WALFORD'S MOST INTIMATE AND PERSONAL PROBLEMS...

Dear Pat,

My life seems to be turning into an episode of *The Jerry Springer Show*. First of all my husband had an affair with his son's girlfriend – a girl half his age and, to be frank, a bit of a scrubber. Then I found myself having a fling with her brother, who turned out to be a total psycho, although on the plus side he knew how to press all the right buttons in the bedroom department. I suppose I realised he wasn't right for me when we ended up attempting to bury my husband alive one night in the woods together. Anyway, now I've been seeing my husband's brother and I'm happier than I have been for a long time. My kids love him too. But, as you can imagine, my ex-hubby wasn't quite so pleased with this new arrangement and was permanently trying to split us up. The whole situation is doing my head in. I'm fed up with having two grown men squabbling over me – what should I do?

Pat says:

I was in a similar situation once, with my third and fourth husbands forever bickering and fighting for my attentions. Even though I'd remarried and moved on, Frank was like a dog with a bone and just wouldn't let go – he even turned up on my doorstep naked once but for a comedy bow tie and those come-to-bed eyes.

Oh how I miss those eyes... However, so far, I have never had to resort to attempted murder. I've wanted to wring Peggy Mitchell's neck a few times, but I don't think I'll be burying her in a casket anytime soon. My advice to you is to find your husband another woman. If he has a new lady in his life by this time next year he'll barely be able to remember your name. So, how old is this husband of yours? I'm single myself at the moment – does he own a comedy bow tie?

'He was naked but for a bow tie and those come to bed eyes!'

Dear Pat,

I'm a pensioner and I share a terraced house with my ever so nice grandson. My problem is that we only have one bathroom and my grandson spends hours in the bath reading his Doctor Who fanzines when I need to pay – well let's just call it a visit. While I don't begrudge anyone a hot soak with a Radox infusion, how can I tell him that at my age when you've got to go, you've got to go? I'm not a woman who's afraid to speak her mind, but when it comes to my waterworks I'd rather not have to discuss them over the breakfast table. I was hoping the Good Lord might have told me how to handle this delicate matter, but he hasn't been in touch so I thought I'd write to you instead...

Pat says:

You should count yourself lucky – there's seven of us living at my house. It's impossible for me to get anywhere near the bathroom and I'm forever tugging ginger hair out of the plughole. I'd suggest leaving your grandson a note to avoid an embarrassing conversation and I'm sure he'd be very understanding. Failing that, knock on the door and ask if he wants any help scrubbing his back. If that doesn't get him out of the bath in a hurry, nothing will.

Dear Pat,

I'd been feeling like a spare part ever since my divorce and hadn't had a proper girlfriend for years – the only bit of action I'd had was with a girl who was helping out at my best mate's wedding. I was bladdered and the next day I couldn't even remember what had gone on or if indeed anything had gone on between us. There's a woman who had a crush on me, but I didn't fancy her in the slightest and the constant whiff

'I'm forever tugging ginger hair out of the plughole...'

'I've never had a shortage of blokes sniffing around me'

You're in the prime of your life and you deserve a bit of lady-loving. When I was your age I never had a shortage of blokes sniffing around me, but things have slowed down of late. Now all I've got for company is a houseful of children and the biggest collection of outsized earrings this side of Walthamstow. It sounds like this young lady just hasn't come to the realisation that you're the one for her. Luv, if you want to get a relationship that will last, don't panic about it – just be yourself!

Dear Pat,

I am a 12-year-old boy and my favourite thing in the whole world is dancing and I even passed my tap exam with a distinction. But when my dad found out I'd been to dance classes without telling him he went mad and now he thinks I'm a sissy. He says boys should do horrible stuff like boxing and that tap dancing is for girls. He wanted to take me paintballing, but I was really worried about getting my glasses dirty. Am I a sissy?

of cheese from her ample cleavage was a right turnoff. I have been in love – she was a cross between someone fit like Jordan and one of them Girls Aloud birds. I proposed to her and even offered to be a dad to her kid, but she just wanted to stay friends. How can I get a girlfriend and keep hold of her? What am I doing wrong?

Pat says:

Of course you're not a sissy, sweetheart! Just look at some of the most famous dancers of our time – Anton Du Beke, Wayne Sleep. What's sissyish about them? Women love a man who knows how to move around a dancefloor and when you're older you'll be a right little heartbreaker. Your dad sounds like something out of the dark ages – tell him you'll go paintballing if he comes to one of your classes and does the cha cha cha.

'I love a man who knows how to move around the dancefloor'

HERE COMES
TROUBLE!

THE
BRAT

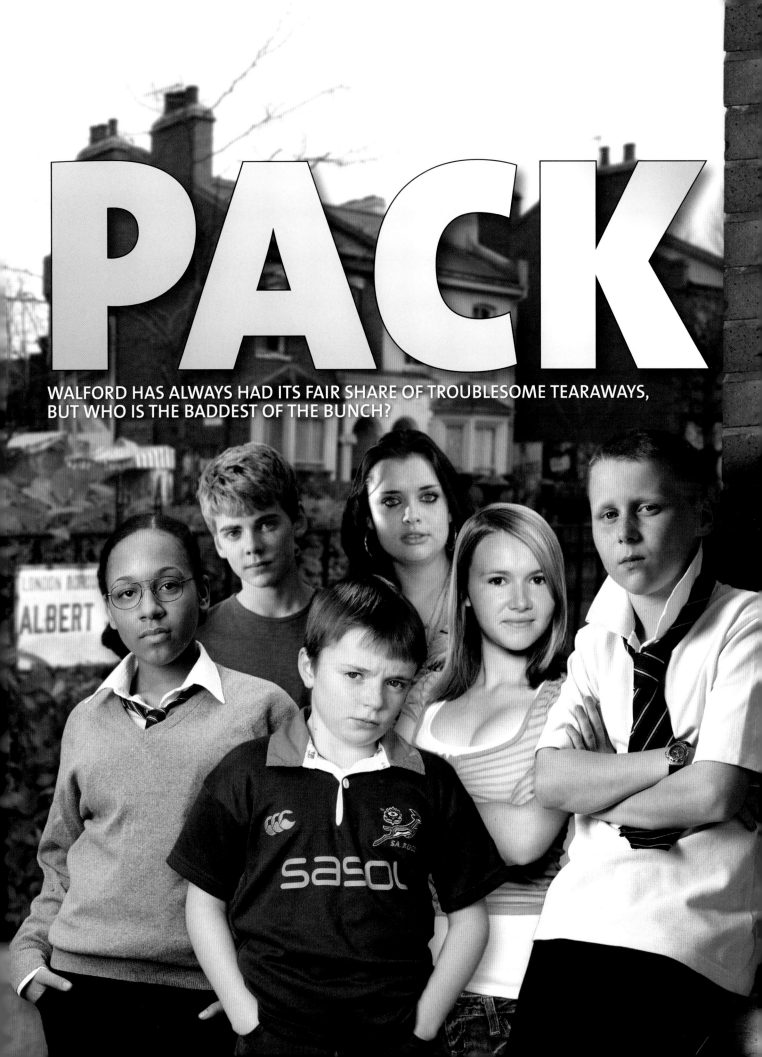

PACK

WALFORD HAS ALWAYS HAD ITS FAIR SHARE OF TROUBLESOME TEARAWAYS,
BUT WHO IS THE BADDEST OF THE BUNCH?

LUCY BEALE

Lucy is proving to be almost as much of a minx as her mother Cindy. The list of offences is pretty impressive – stealing, blackmail, possession of a gun (which loony Steven used to shoot their stepmum Jane), moving crusty boyfriend Olly into her bedroom and a disastrous house party which led to Lucy slapping her dad round the face, resulting in him slapping her back. For that she promised to teach him a lesson once and for all, which she did by disappearing off the face of the earth.

LIAM BUTCHER

Like his dopey dad, Liam probably isn't the brightest spark in Walford, but his heart is in the right place. When he

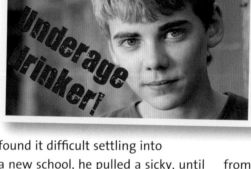

found it difficult settling into a new school, he pulled a sicky, until Ricky found him stuffing his face with chocolate buns and concluded – in a rare moment of intelligence – that maybe his son wasn't ill after all. After a heart to heart, with his dad Liam agreed to go to school, but hid out of view on the swings instead.

PETER BEALE

If Lucy is turning into their mother, then Peter is most definitely a mini-me Ian. In fact he's probably the most sensible person in the Beale household and has yet to break any major rules. Okay he did once drink a stolen bottle of champagne with girlfriend Lauren, but compared to Lucy this budding athlete is a saint.

TIFFANY DEAN

Her butter wouldn't melt exterior betrays a feisty personality she must get from her mum Bianca. So far she's blackmailed her older sister Whitney, stolen a top from Stacey's stall and stuck her tongue out at Zainab Masood before pouring dirty water all over her new window boxes. A chip off the old block!

share of trauma — he was kidnapped by Martin Fowler, nearly drowned in a lake and was terrorised by his dad's psycho fiancée Stella, who poured water onto his bed so Ben would think he'd wet himself, burned his hand, locked him in a garage and broke his hearing aid.

LIBBY FOX

'Squiggle' achieved eight A-stars, two As and a B in her GCSEs. Not bad when you consider that just over a year earlier she'd been kidnapped and drugged by her mad dad Owen who then tried to gas her to death in a stolen car. Libby's only misdemeanours so far have been internet based, thanks to her online scams with boyfriend Darren Miller. The pair also wound up Chelsea by photoshopping images of the beautician and advertising her as a call girl.

BEN MITCHELL

Walford's very own Billy/Benny Elliott would rather be practising his hot shoe shuffle at Wayne De Paul's School Of Dance than roughing up old ladies like his classmate Jay. Not that Ben hasn't been through his fair

LAUREN BRANNING

Lauren has kept herself on the straight and narrow despite getting drunk with Lucy at Jane's hen night and smoking ciggies with Jay Brown when he first arrived in Walford. Lauren was also the catalyst for the Brannings' disastrous Christmas Day in 2007. When she discovered her camera had caught Max and Stacey kissing on film, she burned the footage onto a DVD and planned to give it to Bradley for Christmas. ⟫→

ABI BRANNING

A good friend to Benny Elliott and a self-confessed guinea pig lover, Abi was allowed to choose the name of her new baby brother Oscar. She may appear sweet and sugary, but Abi also has a slightly scary steely side to her personality. She attempted to maim her main rival for the role of Mary in the Christmas nativity play and also destroyed the DVD proving that Max and Stacey had an affair before her parents' divorce hearing.

TAMWAR MASOOD

When nice guy Tamwar first arrived in the Square, Libby Fox hated him because he was the only person at school as clever as her. Unusually for a teen in Walford, he has yet to steal booze or blackmail anyone – he'd much rather be doing gory biology dissections on the kitchen table. Tamwar became an unlikely hero in May when he inadvertently found himself saving the day by catching Whitney as she attempted to rob from Mo's stall. Maybe there's a hunk lurking behind those swotty specs just waiting to be unleashed...

DARREN MILLER

Darren's money-making scams are legendary (who can forget desperaterussianhousewives.com) and it's unlikely Pat Cars would ever have got off the ground without his knack for business. He was also the one who realised that Kevin Wicks was selling dodgy motors – as supplied to him by Phil Mitchell. Darren and Libby finally started a relationship in 2007 over a romantic game of Scrabble. When Darren asked her if they were an item she spelled out 'yes' on the board. Altogether now – aaaaah!

WHITNEY DEAN

The eldest in the Jackson household has been going through a tough time recently – but she remains Bianca's right-hand woman and is like a second mum to the redhead's boisterous brood. Earlier in the year she tried to steal a top from the market stall but was spotted by Mo Harris. She later tried her luck by insisting it was Ricky's fault she was forced to steal because he hadn't given her £20 for a new outfit in the first place!

JAY BROWN

Where do we start? First of all there was the breaking and entering incident at Pauline Fowler's house, swiftly followed by canine kidnapping when he hid Wellard and demanded fifty quid and a games console in ransom. Next Jay shouted racist abuse at Yolande and when his granddad Bert asked him to apologise he mooned instead. This was followed by underage smoking, drinking, fighting, vandalism (the Queen Vic, the Masoods' front wall) and possession of a knife. Then, perhaps worst of all, he terrorised Dot with his teen gang, breaking into her house and smashing it up. However, when gang leader Tegs ordered Jay to throw a brick through Dot's window, he refused. Tegs stabbed Jay which led to Jay testifying against him in court and it finally looked as though the tearaway had turned over a new leaf. But with the murder of his dad Jase, it seems once again Jay may go over to the dark side...

THERE'S NO DOUBT ABOUT IT – CHEEKY CHAV JAY IS THE KING OF THE BRAT PACK!

Gang member!

'Who are you calling a bitch?'

SHE MADE A BRIEF RETURN FOR FRANK'S FUNERAL AND NOW SCHEME-QUEEN JANINE IS COMING BACK FOR GOOD. BUT HAS SHE CHANGED HER WICKED WAYS?

Albert Square has played home to some wicked women over the years. Cindy Beale, Chrissie Watts and Clare Bates have all made a play for the mascara-heavy crown of Walford's Biggest Bitch. But none have quite lived up to the mad, bad reputation of the area's very own teen tearaway turned killer ice queen, Janine Butcher-Evans. A product of her dad Frank's terrible parental skills, and having been dragged from pillar to post as he couldn't quite decide between Pat and Peggy, it was little surprise that Janine evolved into the psycho villainess we know today.

In 2004, Janine left the Square in unceremonious fashion – in the back of a police van, having been wrongfully arrested for the murder

of local frump Laura Beale (who in reality suffered death at the hands of a toy car under her feet at the top of a staircase, not thanks to Janine). Pat knowingly saw her face a life inside for a crime she didn't commit, as payment for her murder of husband Barry Evans, a death she was never made accountable for. Murder wasn't her only pastime – over the years Janine racked up a stunning CV of skills, including prostitution, drug abuse, blackmail and of course seduction.

School's out for teen Janine

A stretch inside awaiting trial ended with Janine walking free after the case fell apart and though she was effectively granted the liberty to exact revenge on Pat, she chose to disappear into the night, not to be heard of again... until now.

Her brief bitchy return to Frank's funeral was a tantalising prelude to a more substantial stint back on Albert Square. With Janine polishing her talons and spying potential victims from the comfort of her swanky sports car, it would've been advisable of the residents to prepare themselves for a hurricane of venom heading back to the Square. Only Ricky and old mate Billy were seemingly safe from Janine's well-stocked supply of hatred.

Now we hear she's coming back to the Square, nobody is safe. Whether they be a local businessman with a bulging bank account, or doormat with a straying husband, Janine's always caused them problems in the past. But has she reformed or will she make Walford pay – big time?

The villainess married Barry Evans in 2003

Fancy a nibble?

WHO NEEDS TO GO UP WEST FOR A NIGHT OUT WHEN YOU'VE GOT THE LIKES OF FARGO'S AND THE QUEEN VIC ON YOUR DOORSTEP. HERE'S OUR GUIDE TO THE FINEST WALFORD CUISINE AND WATERING HOLES. JELLIED EEL ANYONE?

THE QUEEN VICTORIA
46 ALBERT SQUARE
WALFORD

A traditional East End pub in the heart of Albert Square – the perfect venue for a quiet lunchtime pint, a wedding reception or general fisti-cuffs with a family member you've just found out is having it away with your husband/missus. Presided over by landlady Peggy Mitchell, we'd recommend this family-run business for anyone looking for a real taste of cockney London. It was refurbished in July 2007 and recent functions include Heather & Minty's wedding

Mo gets her money's worth at the Vic relaunch

> 'As long as there's the Mitchell name above that door you can be assured the welcome will be as warm as it's always been...'
>
> Peggy Mitchell

Jane gives service with a smile at Kathy's

reception, an open mic karaoke night, a Best Of British Day and the Fishmongers Summer Party – which involved brawling waiting staff dressed as a prawn and a trout. Try the local brew – Thames Bitter Beer.

KATHY'S CAFÉ
2 BRIDGE STREET
WALFORD

This greasy spoon has been the haunt of fry-up-seeking locals for decades. Named after owner

and entrepreneur Ian Beale's late mother, you won't find any of your organic gluten-free mungbean fayre here. At Kathy's we're talking old school hangover food – their fatty bacon sarnies oozing into heavily ketchuped white sliced are the best you'll fine this side of Leytonstone. Environmental Health were called to the establishment last year when competitor Ronnie Mitchell decided to get revenge on Ian following a two

Shirley spices up dinner at the Argee Bargee

for one offer. She released a mouse into the cafe and then proceeded to scream the place down. Ian also kept his dead aunt Pauline's urn there temporarily – but unlike the woman herself, it didn't put anyone off their jumbo sausage.

ARGEE BARGEE
88-90 GEORGE STREET
WALFORD

Offering traditional Indian cuisine, the Argee Bargee's heavenly naan bread is made on the premises and their chilli-tastic King Prawn Vindaloo will make your cheeks redden nearly as much as Bradley Branning's. In fact, it was at this very restaurant that Bradley was about to propose to Stacey – but he collapsed with a nut allergy before he could utter the magic words. Jase did propose to Dawn here, and at Garry's birthday Shirley turned up drunk in Heather's bridesmaid's dress, crashed into the table and fell into Minty's Aloo Gobi, before the whole lot of them were thrown out.

'Since its refurbishment this restaurant has been awarded four stars in the *Walford Gazette* review. We are renowned for our modern take on traditional classics – it is not an audition for *The Jeremy Kyle Show*...'

Maitre d' Bernard when faced with The Jacksons and Jean Slater

FARGO'S
11 LILLY LANE
WALFORD

If you fancy something a bit more Marco Pierre White than Martin Fowler, then Fargo's is the sort of intimate French restaurant every neighbourhood needs. Classy yet informal, it's the place for dates and celebrations – but perhaps not the natural home for the rowdy Jackson brood and Mad Jean Slater, who turned up on Maitre d' Bernard's first day working there. Jean lost the plot when her date Ted didn't turn up and then Ricky and Bianca couldn't afford the bill so poor Pat had to hand over one of her rings as a deposit.

Above: The Jackson brood descend on Fargo's
Below left: Jean loses the plot when she's stood up

But generally it's a romantic setting – thugster Phil and psycho Stella had their first proper date there and Ian and business associate Edward gazed dreamily into each other's eyes as they munched on their coq au vin.

R&R
2-4 TURPIN ROAD
WALFORD

If you can't face getting the vomit-splattered night bus home from Leicester Square, then R&R – previously known as the Market Cellar, Cobra Club, E20, Angie's Den and Scarlett – is Walford's answer to China

The Albert Square singletons strut their stuff at R&R

White's. Owned by the dashing Jack Branning and equally glamourous Ronnie Mitchell, the venue has hosted events such as the local Barmaid Of The Year competition, Heather's hen night (attended only by Heather, Shirley, a gatecrashing Roxy and a fat George Michael lookalike) and a teeny birthday disco which ended with violent hair-pulling between on-off bezzies Lauren and Lucy. Check out local press for the club's different theme nights, but if you're on the pull, be prepared to meet most of your neighbours in there!

BEALE'S PLAICE
15 TURPIN ROAD
WALFORD

There's nothing nicer than eating your soggy chips off last week's *Walford Gazette* is there? This chippy is a local institution and you know what they say – if the locals eat there then it must be worth a try. Whilst the battered cod might be this takeaway's speciality, it's worth going in just to witness the dysfunctional family that work behind the counter

– most notably snivelly owner Ian Beale (yes, him again) and his sulky teenage sprog Lucy. Watching them bitch at each other is easily worth the price of a pickled onion.

MASALA MASOOD
BRIDGE ST MARKET
WALFORD

If you're bored by limp tasteless sarnies why not try something spicier of a lunchtime at Masala Masood, the most recent addition to Walford's foodie scene. Their fragrant 'Curry On The Go' is sensational – even more incredible when you consider that only a couple of months ago chef Zainab Masood had never actually cooked a meal in her own kitchen!

The Masoods decline Ian's business proposal

mad for it

Name: Stella Crawford

Victim: Ben Mitchell

Reign of terror: September 2006 – July 2007
The wicked witch of Walford's hate campaign began with a trip to the London Dungeon, where she abandoned a terrified Ben in the Hall of Mirrors. Next she tore up his Mother's Day card to his gran Peggy, blaming it on Abi Branning, burnt the back of his hand with a boiling hot spoon and dropped his hearing aid into a glass of orange juice, muttering to herself about 'that little freak'. She poured water into Ben's bed so he thought he'd wet himself, smashed up his toys and used to sneak into his room at night and pinch him until he bruised. Once she badly disfigured herself by repeatedly banging her forehead against a wall in a bonkers rage - a pretty sure sign that someone is a total fruitcake.

Maddest moment: On her wedding day, when Ben spluttered that he didn't want her as his new mum, she scratched her fake nails into his chest until blood seeped through his shirt.

Comeuppance: Ben plucked up the courage to speak out, leading to a rooftop confrontation between Phil and Stella. She jumped and died instantly when she splatted onto the bonnet of their wedding car.

Loon rating: 10/10 *Total fruitcake?*

Name: Steven Beale

Victims: Ian Beale, Jane Beale, Lucy Beale, Pat Evans

Reign of terror: September 2007 – May 2008
From the moment he returned to Walford, it was pretty clear that Steven had lost the plot. First of all he pretended to be his dead mother (hello – issues!) and held his 'dad' hostage for weeks. He then shot stepmother Jane in the stomach, leaving her unable to have kids, destroyed his own stall with a piece of scaffolding and tried to end it all by dowsing The Arches in petrol. He accused Christian of coming on to him and then didn't bother telling any of his frantic family that he knew where runaway Lucy was – whilst brainwashing his half sister, saying they'd forgotten all about her.

Maddest moment: Trying to smother his nan Pat as she lay in a hospital bed. As Pat chomped on the pillow her devoted grandson wept as he told her how much he loved her.

Comeuppance: When Ian found out Steven's true evilness, he told the mop-topped loon that if he ever returned to Walford – he'd kill him.

Loon rating: 9/10 *Mop-topped loon...*

Name: Sean Slater

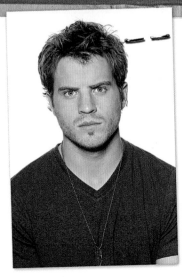

Victims: Gus Smith, Chelsea Fox, Max Branning, Johnny Allen, Jake Moon

Reign of terror: August 2006 onwards
He dug the ditch to help Tanya bury Max alive – although bizarrely during that escapade he actually appeared borderline sane. It's when the eyes go mad and the crazed half smile appears that you have to worry about what Sean's going to do next. Highlights include cutting off Chelsea's hair while she was asleep as revenge for sending him to prison, dating Ruby Allen for her money and bullying Mickey Miller. He didn't take the news he was going to be a dad that well either. Did he go and buy a pair of cute booties? No, he kidnapped his bipolar mum Jean and took her on a terrifying ride in Charlie's cab instead.

Maddest moment: Tying up and gagging poor Gus – possibly the nicest, most inoffensive bloke in the Square – with the intention of killing him and making it look like suicide.

Comeuppance: We're still waiting! Let's just hope Sean will be getting what's due to him sooner rather than later...

Loon Rating: 8/10 Crazed nutter.

Name: Dr May Wright

Victims: Dawn Swann, the Millers, Naomi Julien

Reign of terror: September 2006 – June 2007, June 2008
Unable to have her own children, when May found out Dawn was pregnant after an affair with her husband Rob, she offered to buy the baby. As her behaviour became increasingly erratic, she started popping her patients prescriptions herself, framing Naomi for the missing medication when the nurse realised what was going on. She then attempted to abduct baby Summer from the hospital. Now an even more unstable figure, Mad May returned this year, still desperate to get her hands on Summer, and blew up the Miller house with Dawn and Mickey inside.

Maddest moment: That would be the time she lured a pregnant Dawn to an empty house and drugged and handcuffed Ms Swann to the bed before attempting to perform a caesarean section on her. As you do!

Comeuppance: Her scheming ways were terminated when she managed to kill herself – going out with a bang while blowing up No 27.

Loon rating: 9/10

Demented doctor!

Let's not forget this loopy lot...

Sarah Cairns – Martin Fowler's deluded stalker who threw herself in front of a car, stabbed Martin and pushed Pauline off a ladder – actually maybe she wasn't that barmy after all?

Trevor Morgan – a violent mind-game-playing bully who terrorised his ex Little Mo, burnt her with an iron and destroyed all her self-confidence.

Janine Evans – murdered Barry by shoving him off a cliff the day after their wedding. Well, a night of passion with Barry would be enough to push anyone over the edge...

Glad to be Gay!

THERE'S NEVER A MUNDANE MOMENT WHEN CHRISTIAN CLARKE IS AROUND – HERE'S THE LOWDOWN ON WALFORD'S MR POPULAR...

Christian has a ball soaking Ian in the stocks

You've really got to love yourself to hang a huge blown-up canvas of your own pouting mug in pride of place on your living room wall – an interior design touch that leaves us in no doubt that gym-bunny Christian Clarke thinks he's the best thing to happen to Walford since Jack Branning started taking his shirt off on a regular basis.

There hasn't been an 'omosexual in E20 since interior designer Marco Bianco helped Peggy revamp the Vic. But, unlike that teary twosome, Jane Beale's cocky brother is more than a little bit glad to be gay and as a result there's never been a mundane moment in Walford since he pitched up in January this year.

Christian's name first cropped up when Jane promptly chucked an invitation to her estranged brother's civil partnership in the bin, making it perfectly clear that this was one pair of siblings who weren't exactly from the 'Roxy & Ronnie Joined At The Hip' school of family life. Thinking he knew best, Ian invited Christian and his partner Ashley to Fargo's, where the reason for Jane's lack of enthusiasm for her brother became clear when a very drunk Christian revealed he'd once made a pass at Jane's first husband.

The next day an apologetic, penniless and homeless Christian reappeared – sugar daddy Ashley had thrown him out and the wedding was off. Jane reluctantly allowed Christian to move in to No 45 and then it was up to Ian to get his head around living with a gay man. He was convinced that if Christian had fancied Jane's first husband he'd be next on the list – until Jane pointed out that perhaps he wasn't quite muscle-Mary Christian's type. That hasn't stopped Christian mercilessly winding his panicked brother-in-law up on a regular basis but the whole family has become closer and Ian and Christian even set up their own successful catering business together – Fit For A Queen.

Stroppy niece Lucy is also a Christian fan and at one point he was even chatted up by Roxy – a woman who knows a decent pair of pecs when she sees them – but the penny dropped when Christian pointed out the male stripper he'd organised for Jane was actually an ex-boyfriend and the no-nonsense pair went on to become bezzies.

Steven lied about Christian making a move

One person that wasn't in the Christian fan club was a confused Steven Beale who didn't like the fact that Christian could see he was clearly more into Chase Crawford than he would ever be into Stacey Slater. Steven lied that Christian had made a move on him, leaving the chiselled one with no choice but to quit the Square. However, when it turned out Steven was a loon living in his own fantasy world – and an avid reader of 'bodybuilding' magazines – Christian was thankfully welcomed back into the bosom of the Beale family to continue spicing up Walford life!

NUMBER 1 FAN!

There have only ever been two real loves of Heather Trott's life – stubbly popstar George Michael and creamy chunks of cheese. But which does she fantasise about the most? We investigate...

George Michael v Cheese
The Debate

George facts:
- His real name is Georgios Krylacos Panayiotou
- George wrote Careless Whisper – Heather's fave – when he was 17, but didn't release it until four years later.
- His favourite colours are brown and orange

Cheese facts:
- There are over 700 different varieties produced in Britain
- Cheddar is the nation's most popular cheese
- A 1,400-year-old piece of cheese was unearthed in Tipperary in Ireland. It was still edible

'Every song George's ever written is etched on my heart'
Heather on George

'It's better than sex!'
Heather on cheese

THE CASE FOR AND AGAINST...

I'm Your Man makes you want to swing those hips	You can't dance to cheese
Club Tropicana - drinks are free...	Cheese never bought anyone a drink
George was in teenage girls' dreams circa 1985	Cheese gives you nightmares
It's unlikely Heather is ever going to get her chops around George	Cheese is readily available for munching
George is only ever bright orange	Cheese can be many shades from very pale yellow to bright orange
Jesus To A Child	Cheeses To A Child
Too Funky	Too chunky
'Let's go outside, in the sunshine...'	Taking cheese outside, especially in the sunshine, will only add to its rancid odour and rapid melting

The Verdict

I CAN'T CHOOSE - I LOVE THEM BOTH TOO MUCH! HOW ABOUT GEORGE MICHAEL NAKED AND COVERED IN GORGONZOLA? THAT WOULD BE MY DREAM COME TRUE!

Heather on her hen night – finally meeting her idol?

WALFORD
TOTTY
Sean
Slater

WALFORD
TOTTY
Roxy
Slater

The Walford

HAVE A GO AT OUR BUMPER CROSSWORD!

28 Garry ___, mechanic and Minty's best pal, with a real eye for the ladies (5)

29 3D's grandson, who grew up in South Africa with mum Kathy (3)

31 ___ Fox, Walford beautician who spent time behind bars (7)

32 & 8A Minute Mart boss whose son Anthony was the first of the family in Walford (7,7)

Down

1 ___ Moon, she was Alfie and Spencer's beloved grandma (4)

2 ___ Mitchell, new face who is Ronnie and Roxy's dad and 3D's brother-in-law (6)

3 ___ Mitchell, Queen Vic matriarch kept on her toes by Phil, 11A and Sam's escapades (5)

4 Heather ___, Shirley's pal who married Minty (5)

5 Kareena ___, Walford teen who was romantically linked to Tariq, Mickey and Juley (8)

6 ___ Fowler, longtime Walford resident who took over the greengrocer's stall once run by Uncle Pete (6)

9 Walford grandma who wed Pete, Frank and Roy (3)

14 ___ Harker, good Samaritan who rescued 9D when her car was stolen by Shirley and 4D (3)

17 Walford businessman who, like 9D, now has four marriages under his belt (3,5)

19 & 21D Mad doctor who terrorised 20A, left empty-handed and came back for more drama (3,6)

23 It's the Square at the heart of the action! (6)

24 Masood __, postman married to the formidable Zainab (5)

25 22A's younger daughter, who wants to be a vet when she grows up (3)

26 He's 25D's baby brother, born just weeks before his parents split up (5)

30 Dot Branning's evil son, who likes to come back from time to time to wreak havoc (4)

Across

7 Real name shared by Mo Harris and Little Mo Slater (7)

8 See 32A

10 5D's older brother, whose gambling became a major problem (3)

11 ___ Mitchell, tough nut who fled the Square for a new life in Rio (5)

12 ___ Fowler, she was Mark's 2nd wife (4)

13 Johnny ___, late gangster and nightclub boss, whose daughter fell for Sean (5)

15 ___ Butcher, Frank's second daughter, who swapped Walford for France (5)

16 ___ Watts, former Queen Vic landlady who gave her name to Sharon's Den (5)

18 Nurse who tempted Sonia away from 6D (5)

20 Dawn ___, glamour girl who tries not to let motherhood stand in the way of a good time (5)

22 ___ Branning, mum whose Christmas was wrecked by her daughter's present to Bradley (5)

27 He's the father of Mickey and 20A, who rekindled his romance with Rosie (4)

Puzzler

TRY THIS WICKED WORDSEARCH...

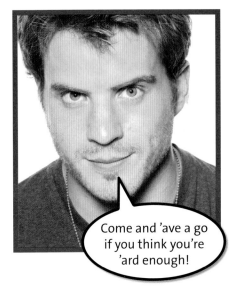

Come and 'ave a go if you think you're 'ard enough!

K	A	S	R	N	O	O	M	T	A	K	S	W	K	S
F	A	L	E	R	O	N	N	I	E	A	C	S	A	K
O	S	R	N	T	D	E	Y	N	A	E	A	A	N	C
J	H	L	E	T	A	X	K	L	E	M	K	R	J	I
A	A	C	O	E	O	B	F	S	M	V	E	A	X	W
S	B	R	H	R	N	I	E	I	A	T	E	B	J	Y
E	N	G	T	R	E	A	T	R	A	Y	E	T	T	L
D	A	R	D	D	I	C	F	L	A	C	K	Y	S	R
Y	M	A	L	E	H	S	S	E	H	L	E	Y	R	A
E	M	N	O	E	N	E	T	E	R	C	C	E	N	C
R	A	T	L	Z	O	N	L	I	A	R	L	K	W	S
N	S	L	O	Z	E	S	I	T	A	N	E	C	A	M
N	O	O	N	A	E	D	S	S	N	N	Y	I	D	E
R	O	L	Y	A	T	Y	L	L	E	K	E	M	R	R
T	D	D	A	N	N	Y	M	O	O	N	H	K	B	A

ALFIE

CARLY WICKS

CHELSEA

CHRISTIAN

CLARE BATES

DANNY MOON

DAWN

DEANO

DENNIS

GRANT

JACK

JAKE

JASE DYER

KAREENA FERREIRA

KAT MOON

KELLY TAYLOR

MICKEY

RONNIE

ROXY

SAM MITCHELL

SEAN

SHABNAM MASOOD

STACEY

STEVEN

ZOE SLATER

ANSWERS ON PAGE 128

SLAP! CAN YOU SPOT THE DIFFERENCE?

Find the eight differences between the two pictures below.

DOT'S EXTREME SUDOKU CHALLENGE

Fill the grid so that every row, every column and every 3x3 box contain the numbers 1–9

2								5
		4	7	6	1		9	2
	1	7					3	
9				7		5	8	3
7	8		1		3			4
6				8				
5		8		1		2		
	3				5	1		
	7	9	2		6			

ALBERT SQUARE BRAINTEASERS!

Are you an intellectual genius like Garry Hobbs or do you have the minimal brain-power of Ricky Butcher? Try these brain-twisting riddles to find out...

1. I can run but not walk. Wherever I go, thought follows close behind. What am I?

2. What five-letter word becomes shorter when you add two letters to it?

3. If you have me, you want to share me. If you share me, you haven't got me. What am I?

4. Throw me off the highest building and I won't break. But put me in the sea and I will. What am I?

5. There is one word in the English language that is always pronounced incorrectly. What is it?

ANSWERS ON PAGE 128

109

This Charming man?

WHAT'S REALLY GOING ON IN THE MANIPULATIVE
MIND OF ARCHIE MITCHELL?

A long-forgotten flame was rekindled this year when Archie Mitchell hooked up with his sister-in-law, Peggy. He was the brother that, deep down, the Queen Vic matriarch wished she'd married instead of Phil and Grant's dad, Eric. Archie – the charming, dapper, clever brother – similarly used to have feelings for Peggy, so when they met up again so many years later perhaps it was inevitable that romance was to blossom.

However, whilst Peggy has been won over by her new fiancé's genuine charms, Archie's motivation is not quite so clear. Was it Peggy he was attracted to or merely the idea of what a relationship with Peggy would bring – the chance to be reunited with his daughters and once again be the controlling head of the Mitchell family? Archie is someone who loves and needs to be in control, but at the same time he's no fool and disguises

this need to be the boss behind a very easy-going facade.

Our first glimpse of Archie's smooth charm was in July when

> Archie is someone who loves and needs to be in control

Ronnie and Peggy travelled to the seaside to find Roxy, who was hiding herself away at her dad's in Weymouth. Whilst Ronnie found it hard to mask her dislike – as we later found out there are some major father/daughter issues going on there – Archie made Peggy feel like a giddy young woman again and she was immediately smitten.

Much to Ronnie's disgust, in a matter of weeks they'd announced their engagement, but she wasn't the only one unimpressed by how quickly her dad had got his feet under the table. A suspicious Phil wasn't too chuffed either, but after all, there is only room for one alpha male in that pub and as far as Archie is concerned the Vic is now very much his territory – and he's the one in charge. He's changed Peggy's look – her new short sensible hair and lady-mayoress blouses have certainlty raised Pat's eyebrows – and he seems to have somehow tamed the irrepressible Ma Mitchell.

Archie may be dressing Peggy like a wife, but will she become the wife? As the power struggle continues, will Peggy get the dream wedding she so deeply craves?

The veteran lovers announce their engagement

Walford Death Map

WHEN IT COMES TO DROPPING DEAD THE RESIDENTS OF E20 HAVE A TEND TO DO IT ON THEIR OWN DOORSTEPS. SO PLEASE WEAR BLACK AND BE SUITABLY RESPECTFUL AS WE LOOK BACK ON 10 YEARS OF WALFORD CORPSES...

TOM BANKS
01.11.02
The Irish firefighter (and fiancé of 'Black Widow' Sharon) was already expecting to die from his recently discovered brain tumour. But his end came a few weeks earlier than expected while attempting to rescue Little Mo and Trevor Morgan from a house fire.

TREVOR MORGAN
01.11.02
The Scots psycho started a fire at the Slaters with Little Mo inside - but ended up killing himself when the flames ignited a can of engine oil.

DEN WATTS
18.02.05
Walford's slimiest resident was killed by Pauline Fowler's dog-shaped door-stopper as wielded by his bonkers big-haired wife Chrissie. Dirty Den was then buried under concrete in the pub's cellar only to be dug up in August that year by a pickaxe-swinging Sam Mitchell.

MAY WRIGHT
18.6.08
While singing along to the music box she'd bought baby Summer, Mad May switched on the oven full blast, lit a cigarette and bang - the Miller's house exploded and before you could say 'Mad As A Spoon' the deranged doc was being carried out in a body bag.

DENNIS RICKMAN
30.12.05
Dennis was stabbed - on the orders of enemy Jonny Allen - as he crossed the Square to meet a pregnant Sharon and start a new life together in the USA. As the New Year fireworks exploded in the sky, Dennis died in Sharon's arms a few steps away from the taxi in which he planned to escape his life of crime.

PAULINE FOWLER
25.12.06
Having alienated everyone around her Pauline had planned to leave the Square and live with Meeeeechelle in the States - but she collapsed and died by Arthur's bench. A combo of the slap she'd just received from Sonia and the saucepan attack from Joe were thought to be to blame.

AUDREY TRUEMAN
06.09.01
Audrey was hit on the head by falling stones as she walked past a building site. A few days later, after a row with wayward son Paul, she collapsed and died. It was at her funeral that the residents of Walford first set eyes on her estranged husband, charmer Patrick...

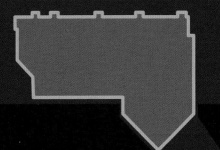

LAURA BEALE
30.04.04

After a vicious cat-fight with Janine in which she was nearly strangled, an emotional Laura Beale died while rushing to answer the front door to estranged hubby, Ian. She tripped over one of Bobby's toys on the stairs, breaking her neck as she fell.

JOE MACER
26.01.07

After admitting he'd whacked his late wife Pauline over the head with a frying pan (well, who wouldn't?) - Joe struggled with Jim and Dot before falling out of an open upstairs window, crashing into a market stall as he died.

JASE DYER
28.8.08

The softly spoken odd-job man was killed in his own flat on the eve of his wedding to Dawn by evil gangland boss Terry Bates - who wanted revenge on Jase for daring to leave the old firm and go straight.

ASHLEY COTTON
14.06.01

After an argument in the Vic, Dot's grandson stole Mark Fowler's motorbike and raced around the Square - unaware his dad Nasty Nick had slashed the bike's brakes in the hope of killing Mark. Oh the irony...

ETHEL SKINNER
07.09.00

Dot's party-girl best friend had terminal cancer and with only months to live a frail Ethel wanted to die with dignity and asked for Dot's help. On the night of her 85th birthday (it was actually her 86th, but she'd always lied about her age), after blowing out the candles on her cake and bidding Dot an emotional farewell, Ethel took an overdose of her pills and died in her sleep.

SASKIA DUNCAN
14.02.99

Steve Owen's stalker ex-girl-friend was bashed on the head with a killer ashtray on Valentine's Day. Matthew Rose and Steve buried her body in Epping Forest, but Matthew was jailed when Steve set him up.

NANA MOON
16.12.05

The much-loved and dotty pensioner had been diagnosed with an aneurysm earlier in the year. While putting the finishing touches to the angel on the top of their Christmas tree, Alfie turned back to his grandmother, who had peacefully died on the sofa.

ROY EVANS
17.03.03

Stress got the better of the Viagra-loving car salesman when he discovered Pat had been covering up an affair between his son Barry's wife Natalie and Frank's son Ricky. Roy believed that Pat had once again chosen Frank over him - leading to his second and fatal heart attack.

113

The Queen Victoria ∞ Photo Album ∞

Yodelay-ee-hoo! Roxy and Ronnie go pigtail crazy after their skiing holiday in Austria

When I'm sixty-five! Birthday girl Peggy makes a wish...

The Queen of the Vic celebrates her big day in style!

Loads of laughs — and fun and games with a giant cucumber — on Denise's hen night!

Aaah memories — Tanya and Max in happier times

The temperature's rising for lucky Minty on his stag night!

Red Nose Day — even Ian and Charlie see the funny side

Thirsty work!
Poor old Jane can't
'bear' it any longer

Heather's looking
for love without
much success

The only
things being
pulled for
Ricky and
Mickey on
Singles' Night
are the pints

Mystic Mo

ROMANCE, A LOTTERY WIN OR A CLIP ROUND THE EAR – WHO KNOWS WHAT THE FUTURE HOLDS FOR THE RESIDENTS OF WALFORD? OUR VERY OWN FORTUNE TELLER MYSTIC MO PEERS INTO HER CRYSTAL BALL TO SEE WHAT'S IN STORE OVER THE COMING MONTHS...

CROSS MY PALM WITH SILVER AND I'LL TELL YOU EVERYTHING - NO REFUNDS!!!

A confused young lady should avoid people who are pretending to be something they are not!

A holiday romance is in store for this charming man... he should just be himself

A blonde beauty should beware of a brother – he's not what he seems

This man had fallen in love...but he should be careful – the future's not a happy one for him

This father's lies will come back to haunt him – and it's all going to end in tears

One female resident's life is turned upside down with a blast from the past

A handsome young man should accept a strange offer...who knows who he might meet?

This mother wants the best for her child...but she should be careful not to interfere

This talented youngster will have their chance to succeed...but they should avoid any surprises!

This proud business woman should remember that honesty is the best policy...before a white lie gets out of hand

This family man should watch his wife more closely – she has a secret

An unlikely couple share a moment of passion that surprises them both

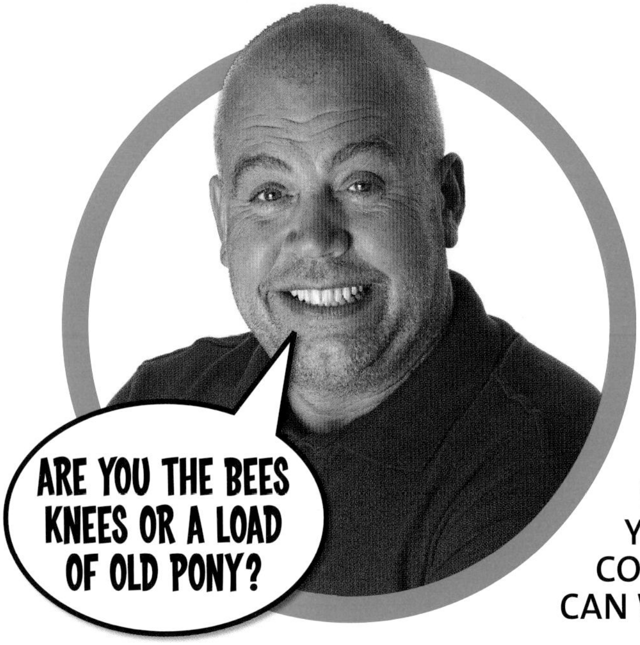
ARE YOU THE BEES KNEES OR A LOAD OF OLD PONY?

Minty's Guide To Cockney Rhyming Slang

DO YOU KNOW YOUR APPLES AND PEARS FROM YOUR DOG AND BONE? HAVE A GO AT MINTY'S COCKNEY RHYMING SLANG QUIZ AND SEE IF YOU CAN WORK OUT WHAT THE 'ECK HE'S ON ABOUT...

Test yourself!

All you have to do is work out which rhyming slang phrases these pictures represent...

'It all went a bit  yesterday. I met this bird in the Vic – the 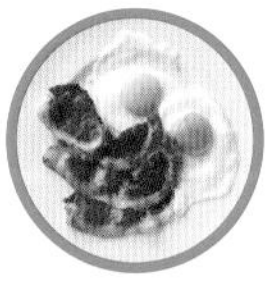 on her went up to here and she had the  of a model. Anyway, we were having a good old  and a  about this 'n' that and I was going to ask her if she fancied a   later. But when I got back from having a  in the Gents she'd vanished. I couldn't  it – I'd bloomin' well bought her  and  all night!'

Oi geezers! Try this bit of lingo if you want to sound like a proper local next time you're headin' daaan Walford way...

Billie Piper = windscreen wiper
'It's peeing it down – you wanna get your Billies on.'

Quentin Tarantino = vino
'Tanya luv, fancy a large glass of Quentin?'

Davina McCall's = balls
'Shirley kneed me right in the Davinas!'

Ronan Keating = central heating
'Turn the Ronan down luv – it's like an oven in here!'

Sara Cox = socks
'Garry, is that stench coming from your Sara's?'

Ricky Gervais = face
'Cor blimey – did you see the Ricky on her?'

Answers: Pete Tong = wrong; Bacon & eggs = legs; Boat race = face; Giraffe = laugh; Rabbit = chat; Ruby Murray = curry; Bruce Lee = wee; Adam & Eve = believe; Britney Spears = beers; Winona Ryder = cider

WALFORD TOTTY

Chelsea Fox

LUCY BEALE:
Teenage kicks

When troublesome teen Lucy Beale decided she wasn't getting enough attention from her dad Ian she threw a boozy house party — announcing it to 357 friends online (see opposite). Needless to say, the place was trashed, Ian slapped his daughter in anger and Lucy promptly ran away, ensuring very quickly that she got her dad's full attention. From that moment on all the frantic Beale clan could talk about was Lucy's whereabouts and — as the months passed — Ian, Jane and Peter just prayed she was still alive. It turned out she was fine and living in a caravan with a load of old hippies and that deranged loon Steven had known where she was all along. Luckily, her bonkers half-brother's plot to run away with Lucy to France via Eurostar was foiled and the teen minx was soon back in Walford in the bosom of her family and causing just as much trouble as before...

myvirtual**desktop**

View Lucy's Friends (357)

Send Lucy an email

Nudge Lucy

▼ Mutual Friends
4 friends in common   See All

Lauren Branning   Peter Beale   Steven Beale   Christian Clarke

▶ Friends
357 friends   See All

▼ Groups
20 groups   See All

Lucy is a subscriber to these groups

My dad stinks of haddock • Which spoilt celebrity are you? • 'I'm a twin – get over it' • 'Danny Dyer is FIT society' • Leave Amy Winehouse Alone! • Walford High is a toilet • We hate girls in Ugg boots • Gay uncles rule!! • High School Musical makes me hurl • I hate fish & chips • I hate parents who treat me like a kid • Belly button piercings are HOT • My brother's a dork • We Love Lily Allen • I hate nosey parents • Are you an inny or outy? • Say NO To Killing Animals 4 Fur!!! • EXAMS SUCK • For All Those Who Truly Have An Evil Stepmother • Battered sausage = wrong!!!!!

▶ Photos
2 albums See All

Mates n Stuff   Christmas 2007:
Jan 2008   Wot a yawn!

Lucy Beale
Lucy Beale is hating her dad and wishing her stepmum would drop dead
Updated 19 minutes ago

Networks:	Walford
Sex:	Female
Interested in:	Boys
Relationship status:	Single
Hometown:	Walford, London
Birthday:	December 9, 1993

▼ Mini-Feed
Displaying 5 messages   See All

Yesterday

 Lucy and Christian Clarke are now friends 6.31pm

March 11

 Lucy joined the group i hate parents who treat me like a kid
11.14pm

March 10

 Lucy added the Which Member Of My Chemical Romance Are You? application 8.29pm

March 8

 Lauren Branning tagged Lucy in a photo 4.50pm

March 8

 Lucy became a fan of Torchwood 2.34pm

▼ The Wall
Displaying 5 messages   See All

Lucy Beale (Walford) wrote
at 10.41pm on March 13th, 2008

 Party at mine. 45 Albert Square, Walford E20. Sunday from 12pm. Bring booze. Everyone invited. This is going to be 1 to remember!

Lauren Branning (Walford) wrote
at 5.50pm on March 12, 2008

I'm lovin that pic, Luce! LOL! ps My mum is acting really weird - am in my room keeping well out of it

Peter Beale (Walford) wrote
at 4.23pm on March 11, 2008

 Give me my ipod back. You are so annoying! Buy your own or maybe just see if it's okay with me b4 you nick my stuff next time if that's not too much to ask?

HOROS

Sagittarius

NOVEMBER 22 – DECEMBER 21

This year could've been tailor-made for you. Ask the right questions and you should get results.

LOVE

The glow around your personal life has to be seen to be believed. Get ready for a springtime high, but bear in mind your high living may leave you feeling jaded.

WORK & MONEY

A fantastic career opportunity comes your way at the end of January. If you let it pass there will be a second chance in March. Use any spare cash for a long-term travel plan.

WALFORD BIRTHDAY: MINTY PETERSON

Capricorn

DECEMBER 22 – JANUARY 19

Things will become so much easier for you when luck plays an important part.

LOVE

An event will take place which could change the direction of your life forever. Keep your eyes open and look around you. Long-awaited names from your past take up the beginning of the year. It will soon become clear why you need to pay attention to them.

WORK & MONEY

Since time began you've struggled to reconcile a career with family. Look out for opportunities to branch free.

WALFORD BIRTHDAY: PHIL MITCHELL

COPES

BEALE OR WILL YOUR LOVE LIFE BE AS COMPLICATED AS JACK BRANNING'S?

Aquarius

JANUARY 20 – FEBRUARY 18

If travel has been high on your agenda, this is the year to make the most of your options.

LOVE

An event will take place in the autumn which could change the direction of your life forever. Keep your eyes open and look around you.

WORK & MONEY

By the end of the year you'll be doing a different job or we'll eat our designer hats! Get ready for a fresh start – it's the biggie you've been waiting for.

WALFORD BIRTHDAY: DENISE WICKS

Pisces

FEBRUARY 19 – MARCH 20

There were times last year when Pisceans could leave everything to Lady Luck and get away with it. Not so this year – she's going to need some help from you.

LOVE

The dreamer in you is praying for a miracle in your personal life. Dream on...The only way your love life will change is for you to give it a helping hand.

WORK & MONEY

The presence of conflicting planets in your house of finance spells trouble, but there's no need to panic. Batten down the hatches and all will be fine by the second half of the year.

WALFORD BIRTHDAY: GARRY HOBBS

Aries

MARCH 21 – APRIL 19

Temperatures run high this year and you'll need to make sure you keep a cool head at all times or others may take advantage.

LOVE
After months of indecision you can feel the sexual tension crackling in the air. The buzz of this will be noticed by your friends all year long.

WORK & MONEY
July and August will see some long-awaited investment (either in the work place or financially) come to fruition. Enjoy it for once!

**WALFORD BIRTHDAY:
YOLANDE TRUEMAN**

Taurus

APRIL 20 – MAY 20

You will take the new year by the horns and set off on a thrill ride of a lifetime, facing down any challenges January throws at you with renewed focus.

LOVE
A few 'lively' conversations in February, May and June with those close to you mean you'll get your own way at last about something that has been troubling you.

WORK & MONEY
Commit yourself to saving more, no matter how tough it may be on your social life! July will be a great month to make a long-term investment.

**WALFORD BIRTHDAY:
CHARLIE SLATER**

Gemini

MAY 21 – JUNE 21

Be excited! New ventures and interests will change your life for the better, so let opportunities into your life and enjoy the ride.

LOVE
You will have a better understanding of where you are heading emotionally. It's time for you to breathe and relax.

WORK & MONEY
Whatever you considered normal up until now is going to look weird by the spring. Money and security will flood in if you can just trust your instincts.

WALFORD BIRTHDAY: ZAINAB MASOOD

Cancer

JUNE 22 – JULY 22

Optimism is the way forward – repeat this to yourself at least five times a day! This phrase was invented for Cancerians in 2009.

LOVE
You've mistreated some people who are close to you so it's time to repair the damage now. It will make your love-life better – we promise.

WORK & MONEY
You know your work situation could be improved. If it's non-existent find something that you love to do and if it makes money – all the better. Watch your finances carefully in October.

WALFORD BIRTHDAY: RONNIE MITCHELL

Leo

JULY 23 – AUGUST 22

To the outside world right now you look very conventional. Stand by to let the mask slip and explore your wilder side.

LOVE

You've been behaving like an angel, but underneath that angelic exterior you've got an itch to rebel, so find a way to do it. March heralds the start of an exciting new era for you.

WORK & MONEY

In June you are likely to be offered something highly lucrative and a lot of fun. It may take you in a new direction. Run with it.

WALFORD BIRTHDAY: LIBBY FOX

Libra

SEPTEMBER 23 – OCTOBER 23

Adjusting to change is not high up on your list of favourite things to do, however if you let someone else invade your privacy, you might find you enjoy it.

LOVE

Romance has been sidelined for you of late. This year your new life comes signed, sealed, delivered. But you'll have to commit yourself – there can be no more hesitation.

WORK & MONEY

You are very well thought of in your job but don't take the future for granted. Start planning your next moves now.

WALFORD BIRTHDAY: SHABNAM MASOOD

Virgo

AUGUST 23 – SEPTEMBER 22

Take your time over delicate areas in your life. The times they are a-changing and you need to change with them.

LOVE

Home routines may come to a head in September and October. Please do the right thing and give yourself and a loved one a weekend way.

WORK & MONEY

Your bank account is suffering so you need to keep a careful eye on your next chance of promotion at work. Work progress is there, but you need to ask for it.

WALFORD BIRTHDAY: BRADLEY BRANNING

Scorpio

OCTOBER 24 – NOVEMBER 21

Accept your friends, family or colleagues for who they are. The fighting has to stop!

LOVE

So much energy has gone into the tricky business of getting your life sorted out. Now it's time for you enjoy yourself – you know you want to...

WORK & MONEY

Spend the first three months of the year building bridges with colleagues and you'll find help comes from an unlikely quarter. You'll have financial concerns in February, but they'll be sorted in time for some summer-time fun.

WALFORD BIRTHDAY: STACEY SLATER

Wishing you a *Merry Christmas* and a *Happy New Year*

GEROUTTA MY PUB!!!

From everyone in Walford!

Walford Puzzler – solutions

CROSSWORD

Across: 7 Maureen, 8 Trueman, 10 Ash, 11 Grant, 12 Ruth, 13 Allen, 15 Diane, 16 Angie, 18 Naomi, 20 Swann, 22 Tanya, 27 Mike , 28 Hobbs, 29 Ben, 31 Chelsea, 32 Patrick.

Down: 1 Nana, 2 Archie, 3 Peggy, 4 Trott, 5 Ferreira, 6 Martin, 9 Pat, 14 Len, 17 Ian Beale, 19 May, 21 Wright, 23 Albert, 24 Ahmed, 25 Abi, 26 Oscar, 30 Nick

SPOT THE DIFFERENCE

1. Streaks in Peggy's hair; 2. Pat's fingernails; 3. Cupboard handles; 4. Pots on microwave; 5. Microwave timer; 6. Pat's buttons; 7. Keyhole; 8. Peggy's tattoo.

WORDSEARCH

BRAINTEASERS

1. A nose; 2. Short; 3. A secret; 4. A wave; 5. Incorrectly

SUDOKU

2	9	6	8	3	4	7	1	5
3	5	4	7	6	1	8	9	2
8	1	7	5	2	9	4	3	6
9	4	1	6	7	2	5	8	3
7	8	5	1	9	3	6	2	4
6	2	3	4	5	8	9	7	1
5	6	8	3	1	7	2	4	9
4	3	2	9	8	5	1	6	7
1	7	9	2	4	6	3	5	8